HAITI Hope for a Fragile State

The Centre for International Governance Innovation (CIGI) was founded in 2001 to provide solutions to pressing governance challenges. CIGI strives to build ideas for global change through world-class research and dialogue with practitioners, which provide a basis for advising decision-makers on the character and desired reforms of multilateral governance. CIGI's purpose is to conduct research of international significance, and to strengthen the intellectual capacity to understand and propose innovative solutions to global challenges. For more information please visit www.cigionline.org.

HAITI Hope for a Fragile State

YASMINE SHAMSIE and
ANDREW S. THOMPSON, editors

Wilfrid Laurier University Press

WLU

We acknowledge the financial support of the Government of Canada through the Book Publishing Industry Development Program for our publishing activities. We acknowledge the financial support of the Centre for International Governance Innovation.

Library and Archives Canada Cataloguing in Publication Data

Haiti : hope for a fragile state / Yasmine Shamsie and Andrew S. Thompson, editors.

Papers originally presented at the conference Canada in Haiti, held at the Centre for International Governance Innovation, Waterloo, Ont., Nov. 4, 2005.
Includes bibliographical references.
Includes conclusion in French.
ISBN-13: 978-0-88920-510-9
ISBN-10: 0-88920-510-8

1. Haiti—Politics and government—1986—Congresses. 2. Haiti—Economic conditions—1971—Congresses. 3. Haiti—Foreign relations—Congresses. I. Shamsie, Yasmine II. Thompson, Andrew S. (Andrew Stuart), 1975– III. Centre for International Governance Innovation

F1928.2.H295 2006   972.94   C2006-901597-X

© 2006 The Centre for International Governance Innovation (CIGI)

Cover design by P.J. Woodland. Text design by Catharine Bonas-Taylor.

∞
Printed in Canada

This book is dedicated to all who refuse to believe
that Haiti is beyond hope.

Contents

Preface

This study of contemporary Haiti, ably edited by Yasmine Shamsie and Andrew Thompson, derives from a conference on Haiti as a fragile state held at the Centre for International Governance Innovation(CIGI) in Waterloo, Ontario, Canada. The sponsors were CIGI, the Centre for Foreign Policy at the University of Waterloo, the Laurier Centre for Military Strategic and Disarmament Studies (LCMSDS), and the Academic Centre for United Nations Studies (ACUNS). The last two institutions are associated with Wilfrid Laurier University whose press has published this book with remarkable speed and professionalism.

The Haiti conference followed an earlier conference on Afghanistan that explored the Canadian experience in those two troubled countries. We began with the premise that the current Canadian emphasis on the so-called three "Ds"—development, democracy, and diplomacy—required detailed examination in specific cases of Canadian involvement in fragile states. To that end we sought to combine groups who do not normally "conference" together but who have had direct experience "on the ground." We therefore invited donor agencies and the many non-governmental organizations (NGOS) who know those agencies so well. We asked leading academics to comment on the historical, social, and political evolution of the countries. We also asked the Canadian military which has taken part in missions to Haiti several times over the last generation and which has more recently undertaken major missions to Afghanistan. We believe that the blend of the three "Ds" has given our conferences a distinct quality.

This book reflects that distinctiveness in that it avoids the political debates about Jean-Bertrand Aristide that dominate so many conferences and current writings about Haiti. Its focus is the society itself, the sources of difference, the origins of violence, and the possibility of change. The authors know Haiti well, whether as residents, academic analysts, non-governmental activists, and, not least, soldiers who tried to establish the stability that has proven so elusive. We were particularly impressed by the military contribution to the conference and book because we believe it offers a perspective seldom shared with a broader audience or reflected in the media.

The editors are optimistic about Haiti's future despite the abundant evidence of the fragility of the Haitian state. The authors similarly possess hope as well as many fears. CIGI and the LCMSDS are working to extend our analyses of what makes states fragile and what response international institutions and national governments should make to the challenge that fragility presents to international peace and stability. We intend to hold conferences and publish similar papers dealing with other states as well as the general question of what puts states "at risk." The superb work done by the editors of this book and the talented conference organizer Katherine Sage-Hayes has established a high standard for our future efforts. We commend them for their excellence.

Terry Copp
John English

Acknowledgements

Haiti: Hope for a Fragile State is the product of a conference on Canada's current "3-D" (defence, development, and diplomacy) engagement in Haiti, that took place in Waterloo, Canada, in early November 2005. As with any edited volume, this book would not have been possible without the help and support of a number of individuals and organizations.

We would like extend our thanks to Stephen Edgar for agreeing to display his wonderful photographs of Haiti at the conference.

To Patricia Goff, president of the Waterloo Region Branch of the Canadian Institute of International Affairs (CIIA), we offer thanks for organizing Robert Fatton, Jr.'s keynote address to the CIIA.

At the University of Waterloo's Centre for Foreign Policy (CFP), we would like to thank Geoffrey Hayes for co-sponsoring and assisting with the facilitation of the conference.

At the Academic Council on the United Nations Systems (ACUNS), we would like to thank Alistair Edgar and his staff for helping to organize many of the logistical aspects of the conference. Special thanks go to Katherine Sage Hayes who, with the help of two student volunteers, Keren Gottfried and Stefanie McKinnon, worked tirelessly to see that all participants were looked after and that the conference was a success.

To Terry Copp and his staff at the Laurier Centre for Military Strategic and Disarmament Studies (LCMSDS), we would like to extend our gratitude for not only proposing the idea of a conference on Haiti in the first place but also for helping to shape the agenda and for securing funding for the conference. On this note, we would like to acknowledge the generous support that we received for the conference from the Canadian Department of National Defence Strategic Defence Fund.

Special thanks are in order for John English and the staff at the Centre for International Governance Innovation (CIGI). It was Dr. English who suggested that the conference papers be turned into a book; it was his support and encouragement that made this suggestion a reality.

To Dan Latendre and his staff at IGLOO, especially Juanita Metzger, thank you for producing *HaitiConnect,* the digital research portal that will allow academics, practitioners and non-governmental organizations to access, share and disseminate their research on Haiti.

Brian Henderson, Jacqueline Larson, Clare Hitchens, and Carroll Klein at Wilfrid Laurier University Press also deserve special praise for going to great lengths to accommodate our request to expedite the book's release.

Finally, we would like to thank all of the authors who contributed to the book. As we're sure all who read the book will find, their insights into the current challenges that Haiti must overcome are invaluable.

List of **Acronyms**

ACUNS   Academic Council on the United Nations System
AI   Amnesty International
AORS   Areas of Responsibility
CAS   Close Air Support
CBC   Congressional Black Caucus
CCIC   Canadian Council for International Co-operation
CEP   Conseil Electoral Provisoire
CF   Canadian Forces
CIDA   Canadian International Development Agency
CIGI   The Centre for International Governance Innovation
CIIA   The Canadian Institute for International Affairs
CNG   National Governing Council
COS   Chief of Staff
CSR   Corporate Social Responsibility
DDR   Disarmament, Demobilization and Reintegration Program
DSRSG   Deputy Special Representative of the Secretary General
EERP   Emergency Economic Recovery Program
FADH   Forces Armées d'Haïti; Haitian Armed Forces
FARE   Fédération des Associations Régionales Étrangères
FAVACA   Florida Association for Volunteer Action in the Caribbean
and the Americas
FC   Force Commander
FDI   Foreign Direct Investment

FIBUA Fighting in Built-Up Areas

FOCAL Canadian Foundation for the Americas

FPUS Formed Police Units

FRAPH Front pour l'Avancement et le Progrès Haïtien; Front for the Advancement of Progress in Haiti

G-184 Group of 184; Groupe des 184

GDP Gross Domestic Product

HNP Haitian National Police

HRC United Nations Human Rights Commission

HTA Haitian Hometown Associations

HUMINT Human Intelligence

ICISS International Commission on the Intervention of State Sovereignty

ICKL Karl Lévêque Cultural Institute

ICF Interim Cooperation Framework

IDB Inter-American Development Bank

IFIS International Financial Institutions

IMF International Monetary Fund

INS Immigration Naturalization Service

IPS Canada's 2005 International Policy Statement

KAIROS Canadian Ecumenical Justice Initiatives

LCMSDS Laurier Centre for Military Strategic and Disarmament Studies

MICAH International Civilian Support Mission in Haiti

MICIVIH Joint OAS/United Nations International Civilian Mission in Haiti

MIF Multinational Interim Force

MIPONUH United Nations Civilian Police Mission in Haiti

MINUSTAH Mission des Nations Unies pour la stabilisation en Haïti; United Nations Stabilization Mission in Haiti

MNF Multinational Force

NCOS Non-Commissioned Officers

NGOS Non-governmental organizations

NOAH National Organization for the Advancement of Haitians

OAS Organization of American States

OAS-DEMOC OAS civilian mission to Haiti

PAPDA Haitian Advocacy Platform for Alternative Development

PDSRSG Principal Deputy of the Special Representative of the Secretary General

ROCAHD Regroupement des organismes canado-haïtiens pour
le développement
SAS Small Arms Survey Project
SIGINT Signal Intelligence
SMES Small Market Economies
SRSG Special Representative of the Secretary General
TF Task Force
TGOH Transitional Government of Haiti
UN United Nations
UNDP United Nations Development Program
UNMIH United Nations Mission to Haiti
UNPOL United Nations Police
UNSCR United Nations Security Council Resolution
UNSMIH United Nations Support Mission in Haiti
UNTMIH United Nations Transition Mission in Haiti
USAID United States Agency for International Development

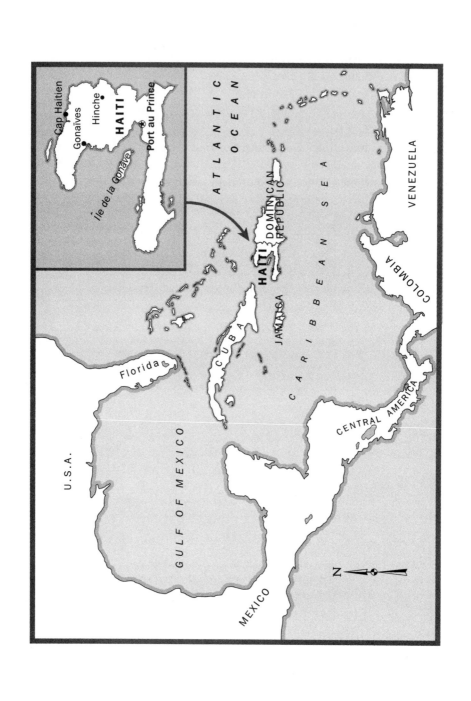

Introduction

Haiti
Hope for a Fragile State

YASMINE SHAMSIE
ANDREW S. THOMPSON

In his book *Collapse,* the American biologist/ecologist Jared Diamond ends his chapter on Haiti and the Dominican Republic by asking whether there is any hope for Haiti.[1] Although pessimistic, it is, unfortunately, a fair question. At present, Haiti is a divided country in the midst of a political, economic, ecological, and social crisis. HIV/AIDS rates are among the highest in the Western hemisphere. Violence, bolstered by the prevalence of thousands of small arms in the hands of both state and non-state actors, has sabotaged attempts to establish the rule of law, leading to an overall climate of insecurity. The transitional government lacked popular legitimacy, and state infrastructure is notably absent in much of the country, particularly in the rural areas. In sum, Haiti is—by most measures—a fragile state.

This book is the outcome of a highly successful conference that took place in Waterloo, Canada, in November 2005.[2] The impetus for the conference was the Haitian insurgency of February 2004 that forced President Jean-Bertrand Aristide to flee the country, precipitating the establishment of a transitional government and prompting members of the international community to intervene militarily for the second time in ten years. The primary purpose of the conference was to discuss how Haiti, with the assistance of the international community, might shed its current distinction as one of the world's failing states. Understandably, the tone of the conference was largely one of pessimism. The challenges that Haiti must overcome are formidable, and there is considerable evidence to suggest that the commitment of outside actors to the tiny island nation will be fleeting.

Nonetheless, the purpose of this book is not to reinforce the popular notion that Haiti is, to quote Diamond, the "modern New World's saddest basket case."[3] Rather, the aims of the contributors are more ambitious, although perhaps counterintuitive. On one level, they are to shed light on the varied and complex roots of the current crisis, dispel misperceptions, and offer possible recommendations for moving forward. Perhaps more importantly, however, the contributors to this volume suggest that the situation in Haiti, despite evidence to the contrary, is not completely desperate. Without question, the task of building a functioning society is a daunting one, as Haiti's immediate future appears bleak and full of peril. Its long-term story has yet to be written, however, and it would premature to write Haiti off as a nation beyond repair. Although the odds seem stacked against Haiti, there is reason to be hopeful.

Haiti as a "Fragile State"

In 1996, in the wake of three-year military coup d'état that interrupted President Jean-Bertrand Aristide's first term in office in the early 1990s, Jean-Germain Gros dubbed Haiti an "anaemic failed state," his assessment being that the state was so "emaciated" that its "archaic structures" and institutions provided the government with little control over the country.[4] Given the turmoil that followed the coup, his metaphor was not inappropriate. Even so, when assessing states that have either ceased to function altogether or have been plagued by high levels of violence, terminology matters. The most common adjectives found in the academic literature used to describe these states include "failed," "collapsed," and "fourth world" states, as well as "failing," "fragile," and "weak" states. Although these terms are used to describe similar conditions and ailments—often interchangeably—the distinctions are important, and act as more than an exercise in semantics. Not only are these adjectives vague and open-ended but how they are employed—and to which states they are applied—is a subjective exercise. Subjectivity is evident in the selection of indicators used to measure a state's functionality and the degree of dysfunction to which a state is believed to have descended. Relying again on a medical metaphor, how a state is perceived, both by its own citizens as well as by the international community at large, reveals a great deal about its "prospects of recovery." There is a pejorative connotation to the first three terms listed above, the implication being that "failed," "collapsed," and "fourth world" states have disintegrated to a point beyond salvation, whereas "fragile," "failing," or "weak" states suggest that the degree of dysfunction in a state has not yet reached the point of complete societal breakdown and that the possibility remains of becoming a "stable," "functioning," and, in time, "strong" state.

As the title of this book suggests, the authors believe that Haiti's destiny lies not with the former set of phrases but with the latter.

Scholars have pointed to a series of key indicators—and this list is by no means exhaustive—that are present, at least on some level, in "failed" and "fragile" states. For Gros, these are "economic malperformance, lack of social synergy, authoritarianism, militarism, and environmental degradation caused by rampant population growth."[5] Included under these headings are related factors such as political parties on the extreme right and left of the political spectrum, state power in the hands of the elite, the absence of a middle class, the ever-pervasive legacy of colonialism, and tension between ethnic and religious groups.[6] To this list one could add, as Robert D. Kaplan has suggested, the emergence of high levels of scarcity, crime, tribalism, and disease,[7] or, as Robert I. Rotberg has argued, the inability to "deliver political goods" such as security, education, and health services to its citizens.[8] More recently, Simon Chesterman, Michael Ignatieff and Ramesh Thakur have argued that the absence of strong judicial institutions and "apolitical bureaucratic structures (civil service, judiciary, police, army) supported by an ideology that legitimates the role of neutral state authority in maintaining social order through prescribed procedures and the rule of law" constitutes a strong indicator of "fragile" status.[9] Nor should the impact of widespread access to small arms, particularly in the hands of non-state actors, be underestimated.[10] To one degree or another, Haiti has suffered, and continues to suffer, from all of these ailments.

The Roots of the Conflict

What caused the tiny island nation to become so fragile? The answer, of course, is far from obvious or straightforward. One of the aims of this book is to offer insight into the unique political, social, economic and cultural forces that are behind Haiti's current predicament. The first section, "The Current and Historical Context," examines the current crisis through the lens of Haiti's troubled past. In the opening chapter, Robert Fatton argues that the roots of the insurrection of February 2004 can be found in "the material and historical circumstances of the colonial period."[11] Specifically, it was the plantation economy, which required a disciplined labour force in order to succeed, that reinforced the authoritarian ruling structures left behind by the French. This, along with the fears that the western powers would attempt to retake control of the country and the "class aspirations of Haitian leaders," has had the effect of entrenching a despotic tradition of rule that all presidents, including Aristide, have perpetuated. Consequently, Fatton concludes that this way of governing is likely to remain the norm for the foreseeable future, with real change dependent on whether "key segments of the Haitian political class will finally realize that they should accept the logic of democracy."

For its part, the international community has struggled to promote democracy in Haiti. In surveying past engagements, Robert Maguire notes that Haiti has come to represent a quagmire for policy-makers in both the United States and Canada. Given both Haiti's geographic proximity, and its significant Diasporas living in North America, officials in Washington and Ottawa cannot ignore the instability that has plagued the tiny island nation. Yet a sustained commitment has been missing, at least at the state level. One reason for this may be that many view Haiti's problems as irresolvable. Maguire disagrees. However, he warns that there can be no "quick fixes." Instead what is needed is "a realistic and objective understanding and assessment of Haiti and its challenges." Among other things, this means that the international community must resist the temptation to exit prematurely; initiate judicial and penal reform in conjunction with police reform; refrain from further weakening state institutions by withholding funds; avoid actions that will exacerbate political schisms; promote peaceful dialogue between factions; and, above all, confront the problems associated with endemic poverty.

It is this last dilemma—tackling the country's oppressive poverty—that has posed the greatest difficulty for foreign donors to Haiti. In her chapter, Yasmine Shamsie examines the limitations and problems associated with previous efforts to craft economic development policy in Haiti. She argues that long-term peace will hinge on the country's ability to address the vast inequalities of economic and political power. Her review of past efforts suggests that the economic development model promoted by international peacebuilding agencies has worsened rather than improved these trends. More specifically, development strategies have been plagued by an urban bias, devoting little attention to rural areas, which has increased both poverty and inequality, jeopardizing political and economic stability.

The Limits of Foreign Intervention

Equally challenging when addressing the problem of fragile states is determining the specific measures needed to promote sustainable development and durable peace. Clearly, the idea that there is an approach to state-building that can be applied more or less universally is simplistic, if not naive. There is nonetheless a general consensus that the ultimate goal is to build "self-sustaining indigenous institutions" that allow for "competent democratic governance and economic growth."[12] How to go about it and who should be responsible are questions where there is understandably little consensus among academics or the international community at large. Some scholars have called for the improved "early warning systems" that allow for preventive responses so that states do not become unstable in the first place. Although a noble aim, it is fraught with problems. As many scholars and practitioners have noted, it often takes a crisis to spur the international community into action. As such, large-scale preventive measures (assuming of course that state breakdown can be predicted) are unlikely to be adopted.

Moreover, international military intervention in the sovereign affairs of fragile states is a contentious issue. The International Commission on the Intervention of State Sovereignty (ICISS), which explored the question of "when, if ever, it is appropriate for states to take coercive—and in particular military—action, against another state for the purposes of protecting people at risk in that other state," argued in its report, *The Responsibility to Protect* (R2P), that coercive interventions would only be justified in situations involving "large scale loss of life" and "large scale 'ethnic cleansing.'"[13] Based on these criteria, it is debatable whether the decisions to intervene militarily in Haiti, either in the mid-1990s or mid-2000s, would have met such a formidable test. Besides, appeals to the conscience of the international community are rarely enough to provoke action. Indeed, since 9/11, the rationales for intervention in failed and fragile states have become increasingly realist in tone, with the bulk of the focus shifting to US-led nation-building efforts in Iraq and Afghanistan. Francis Fukuyama has argued that "the chief threats to us and to world order come from weak, collapsed, or failed states" because of their dual potential to destabilize their neighbours and act as the nexus that brings together terrorist organizations and weapons of mass destruction.[14] Similarly, Michael Ignatieff, who was one of the ICISS commissioners, has noted that "failing states or failed ones that pose no security challenge to vital interests [of the US and UK] are unlikely to be the target of coercive intervention, even when the human suffering inside them cries out for action."[15]

Given Haiti's proximity to the United States, prompting the international community to intervene has not been the problem. Even so, when considering the role that the international community—particularly the United States—might play in Haiti, the twin issues of capacity and "political will" stand out. The latter notion, political will, usually refers to the readiness of the United Nations' (UN) more powerful member states to act in their own interests. More to the point, scholars such as Fukuyama question whether the international community is well-suited for state-building. He contends that the UN and other multilateral organizations lack the "expertise or the resources, human and otherwise, to run nation-building programs authoritatively."[16] Similarly, Marina Ottaway of the Carnegie Endowment for International Peace has questioned whether the international community possesses either the know-how or desire to see state-building initiatives through to the point where indigenous state institutions are self-sustaining and able to provide at least a minimum level of services to their citizens.[17] Taking this idea a step further, Ottaway questions whether establishing a system of democratic rule is a realistic expectation, given that past rebuilding efforts have resulted in a quagmire for donor nations. The implications of this observation are, of course, tremendous. She admits that the alternatives—using aid to entice warring factions into passivity, encouraging regional governments to occupy the area in order to fill the void in governance, or supporting authoritarian leaders who will stabilize the situation—are "unpalatable."[18] To accept these options is to sacrifice both the rights of the state's citizens and the potential for long-term stability in favour of regional order and short-term expediency. That being said, given the costs and duration of nation-building, and the fact that UN missions are notoriously vulnerable to budget cutbacks, she may be correct in suggesting that, at least in some cases, the "unpalatable" outcomes listed above are more likely than the emergence of a vibrant, democratic society. Indeed, as Ignatieff notes, "exporters of liberal democracy have essentially severed the liberal from the democracy, putting exclusive emphasis on frequent multi-party elections and putting almost no emphasis on the rule of law, development of an independent judiciary, and training an honest prosecution service."[19]

The second section of the book, "Justice and Security," examines the challenges involved with any rebuilding effort that makes human security the key priority. Offering a critique of the tenuous place that human rights have had in Haiti over the last half century, Andrew Thompson examines past failures to secure a human rights culture, and suggests that, although difficult, investing in such a culture is necessary for any long-term stability. Col. Jacques Morneau provides an insider's look into the operational and organizational challenges that the UN Stabilization Mission in Haiti (MINUSTAH) has encountered since February 2004. Morneau, the former Commander Task Force Port-au-Prince and Chief of Staff of MINUSTAH, argues that the current UN Mission lacks both the necessary resources and the appropriate authority to provide meaningful security in Haiti. Much of the problem, he argues, rests with conditions on the ground—widespread poverty, high levels of crime, dysfunctional judicial and penal systems, and extensive environmental damage. But he also suggests that the UN Mission has not been set up to meet the expectations placed on it. MINUSTAH's mandate requires that it work along-side the Haitian National Police (HNP)—a force under-staffed, politicized, and prone to both corruption and to committing human rights abuses—in all matters related to policing, an arrangement that has compromised MINUS-TAH's legitimacy. Burdened with an overly bureaucratic United Nations system, poor organizational planning, and insufficient military capacities, the current mission lacks the ability to fulfil its duties and functions. He concludes that the solution, as objectionable as it might seem, could be that Haiti needs to become a "UN protectorate or trusteeship" for a period of ten to fifteen years.

All of the authors in this volume suggest that the international community should neither turn its back on Haiti nor look for easy solutions that will act as the pretense for a premature exit. As this book goes to press, it appears as though international actors have adopted this outlook and committed themselves to staying the course in Haiti, at least for the short-term. On 14 February, one day before MINUSTAH's mandate was scheduled to expire, the United Nations Security Council renewed the mission until 15 August 2006, with the possibility of further renewals if necessary.[20]

This commitment was prompted in part by the turbulent events surrounding the presidential elections of 7 February 2006. After having been delayed four times due to slow voter registration and infighting within the body responsible for organizing the elections, the Conseil Electoral Provisoire (CEP), the voting proceeded fairly smoothly, as Haitians turned out on mass to cast their ballots for the first time in six years. Although plagued by long line-ups, the day was relatively calm and generally free of violence. Initial results indicated that frontrunner René Préval had received roughly sixty per cent of the vote, well over the fifty per cent that a candidate needed in order to be declared the winner on the first ballot. But counting the votes proved to be a cumbersome and difficult task for the organizers. A week after the vote, with still no official announcement, reports emerged that Préval's lead had slipped to approximately forty-eight per cent, meaning a second round of voting would be necessary despite the fact that no other candidate had more than twelve per cent of the vote. Préval's supporters were outraged. They accused the CEP of manipulating the vote, a charge that was bolstered by the discovery of more than 100,000 unmarked ballots that had been included in the overall tally of the popular vote. Mass protests in Port-au-Prince soon followed with threats of widespread violence if Préval was not declared the immediate winner; unfortunately, the calm of the week before appeared to be all but over. Backed into a corner, the CEP wisely conceded. On 15 February, it decided to reject the spoiled ballots, a move that boosted Préval's tally to approximately fifty-one percent, making him Haiti's new President-elect. In doing so, the CEP avoided not only a second round of voting, but also a potentially highly violent situation.

While significant, on its own the election has done little to resolve the divisions that currently exist within Haitian society. Haiti's political parties are currently deeply fragmented and polarized (a point that Fatton develops in his chapter). Virtually all are weak, and none offer a truly national voice with a discernible political project. Moreover, there is a strong chance that Préval will not have the support of the Haitian Parliament, a prospect that would mean political paralysis for the new government. Shortly before the election, *The Economist* suggested that "the vote will give [Haiti] the new start it needs."[21] However, past elections have neither resolved Haiti's problems, nor altered the behaviour of Haiti's political and economic elite, many of whom have never bought into the idea of representative government.

It remains to be seen whether the international community will attempt to scale-back its presence at the first available opportunity. In 2006, the current mood suggests that prolonged support for Haiti is likely not forthcoming. This feeling may stem from failed efforts in the past to strengthen state-institutions in Haiti. Indeed, there is a real danger that governments will develop a case of "Haiti fatigue," a phrase that has been used to describe the general feeling of cynicism within the international community that has come about as a result of past aid projects that have failed to achieve any lasting effect.

New and Emerging Partners

Luckily, donor governments are not the only actors with a vested interest in seeing Haiti become a thriving country. The third section, "Building Haiti through Civil Society," examines the role that non-governmental organizations (NGOs), both domestic and international, can play in Haiti's development. Carlo Dade of the Canadian Foundation for the Americas (FOCAL) suggests that aid officials and organizations are only now beginning to comprehend the impacts of both private sector development and the remittances from the Haitian Diasporas on Haiti's development. Dade notes that, traditionally, aid communities have not had much experience working with either the Diaspora or the private sector and joint initiatives have been ad hoc and slow to come about. Nonetheless, given that the Diasporas and the private sector together invest more money in Haiti than do all the international governmental aid agencies combined, Dade argues that the gains from these types of public-private partnerships are potentially substantial, and, at the very least, warrant considerably more study from scholars and practitioners.

Still, the activities of NGOs are not without their controversies. At present, the debate surrounding Haiti is plagued by widely divergent voices with differing interpretations of the events that sparked the crisis of February 2004. In his chapter, Jim Hodgson of the United Church of Canada asks the question, "To whom do we choose to listen?" He criticizes certain individuals and civil society organizations on the left, many of whom had been calling for Aristide's immediate return, which see the current crisis solely through the lens of US imperial aspirations, a lens that he believes provides only a partial understanding of the situation, partly because it does not "take seriously the voices of Haitians." Hodgson also has words of caution for the Canadian government. He joins with other representatives of Canadian civil society such as the Canadian Council for International Cooperation (CCIC) and Canadian Ecumenical Justice Initiatives (KAIROS) in reproaching the Canadian government for viewing Haiti through a security rather than a development lens. According to Hodgson, Haiti requires a more sophisticated approach than that advocated in Canada's International Policy Statement (IPS), which views "fixing the state" as the solution to alleviating security threats to Canada. While "fixing" the Haitian state constitutes a worthwhile goal, Hodgson argues that making it "work better" is not sufficient. Over the long term, the state must function to ensure the protection of human rights and to create greater social justice for all Haitians.

Conclusion: Hope for the Future?

Hodgson's message regarding the value and desirability of listening to Haitian voices is one that we have attempted to take to heart in planning this volume. This collection of essays therefore concludes with the contribution of Suzy Castor, Director of Haiti's Centre de Formation et de Recherche Économique et Sociale pour le Développement (CRESFED). Castor is a scholar with a long history of political activism in pursuit of justice and peace in her country. While her chapter thoughtfully traces the historical causes of the current crisis, it is her discussion of the challenges that Haiti currently faces which is particularly noteworthy. Like all who study Haiti, she highlights the challenge of security, and agrees with all the volume's contributors that disarmament and police reform are essential. She is, however, critical of MINUSTAH's earlier efforts to address the security situation. The Mission's lack of success in the slum areas, she suggests, has stemmed from its tendency to view Haiti's violence as largely socially rooted. Recently, the Mission has acknowledged that political motives have also been at work. This bodes well for future efforts, she argues. It also speaks to the need for better intelligence gathering, a concern that Morneau also raises in chapter five. Castor also argues that Haitians must resist the impulse to remedy the country's security problems by re-constituting the Haitian army, which was disbanded under Aristide. The political and human rights implications (not to mention the economic burden) of such a move would be disastrous and would represent a colossal step backward.

It is worth noting that this book is not meant to be a comprehensive analysis of the unique set of circumstances that make Haiti such a compelling case study; more specifically, there are four areas in particular that do not receive the attention they deserve. The first is the influence of the Dominican Republic on the current crisis. The two countries that share the Island of Hispaniola are connected in a variety of ways, and yet there is much that separates the two peoples; to understand Haiti, one must also understand the influence of its neighbour to the east. The second omission is the importance of religion in Haiti, particularly the voodoo religion; in Haiti, faith is a powerful cultural force, and its appeal as a medium through which life is understood should not be underestimated.[22] Third is the impact of HIV/AIDS on Haitian society. According to Harvard physician Paul Farmer, over the course of the 1990s, "HIV surpassed tuberculosis as the leading infectious cause of adult death in Haiti."[23] The problem is further exacerbated by the country's extremely poor socio-economic and health indicators. The fourth omission is the long-term effect of environmental degradation. As many scholars have noted, the country faces substantial environmental pressures from the loss of forests and severe soil erosion. These conditions have substantially reduced the soil's fertility leading to serious implications for rural poverty.

Although a number of chapters point to mistakes that were made in the past as well as aspects of the political and economic systems that are in need of reform, the purpose of the book is not to provide a "shopping list" of solutions for Haiti. When dealing with such questions there is an obvious temptation to be prescriptive; the contributors to this book made a conscious effort not to do so. Haiti's destiny is in the hands of Haitians. While the international community can assist, it cannot assume the burden of governing. Even so, the hope is that this volume will offer some guidance for moving forward, and that it will assist those who are charged with the seemingly overwhelming task of making sure that Haiti's status as a fragile state is as short-lived as possible.

Notes

1 Jared Diamond, *Collapse: How Societies Choose to Fail or Succeed* (New York: Viking, 2005), 341.

2 The title of the conference was Canada in Haiti: Considering the 3-D Approach. It was co-hosted by four academic organizations, all of which are located in the Waterloo area: the University of Waterloo's Centre on Foreign Policy; the Laurier Centre for Military Strategic and Disarmament Studies (LCMSDS) at Wilfrid Laurier University (WLU); the Academic Council on the United Nations System (ACUNS), also at WLU; and the Centre for International Governance Innovation (CIGI).

3 Diamond, *Collapse*, 22.

4 Jean-Germain Gros, "Towards a Taxonomy of Failed States in the New World Order: Decaying Somalia, Liberia, Rwanda and Haiti," *Third World Quarterly* 17, no. 3 (1996): 459.

5 Ibid., 462.

6 Ibid., 462–66.
   On the issue of the role that colonialism has played in state failure, James Maynell has argued that the past "will continue to constrain and shape developments, sometimes in ways that may not be immediately recognizable to the actors themselves. In most parts of the world, language, law, religion and cultural pursuits and pastimes—all those aspects of a nation's life that seem most home-grown and constitutive of a people's identity—will on closer inspection reveal traces of old conquests and long-forgotten foreign influences." See James Maynell, "The Legacy of Colonialism," in *Making States Work: State Failure and the Crisis of Governance*, ed. Simon Chesterman, Michael Ignatieff, and Ramesh Thakur (Tokyo: United Nations University Press, 2005), 57.

7 Robert D. Kaplan, "The Coming Anarchy," *Atlantic Monthly* 273, no. 2 (1994): 44.

8 Rotberg's list of "political goods" includes "security, education, health services, economic opportunity, environmental surveillance, a legal framework of order and a judicial system to administer it, and fundamental infrastructure requirements such as roads and communications facilities." See Robert I. Rotberg, "The New Nature of Nation-State Failure," *The Washington Quarterly* 25, no. 3 (Summer 2002): 87.

9 Simon Chesterman, Michael Ignatieff and Ramesh Thakur, introduction: to *Making States Work*, 2–3, 8. For further elaboration on the idea of the importance of politically neutral state institutions, see Sebastian von Einsiedel, "Policy Responses to State Failure," ibid., 13–35.

10 Rotberg offers a fairly scaled-back definition of a failed state, which he describes as "tense, deeply conflicted, dangerous, and bitterly contested by warring factions." See Rotberg, "The New Nature of Nation-State Failure," 85.

11 For further reading on the historical roots of authoritarianism in Haiti, see Michel-Rolph Trouillot, *Haiti: State against Nation* (New York: Monthly Review Press, 1990); and Michel S. Laguerre, *The Military and Society in Haiti* (Knoxville, TN: University of Tennessee Press, 1993).

12 Francis Fukuyama, "Nation-Building 101," *Atlantic Monthly* 293, no. 1 (January/February 2004): 159, 162.

13 *The Responsibility to Protect*, Report of the International Commission on Intervention and State Sovereignty (Ottawa: IDRC, December 2001), vii, xii.

14 Fukuyama, "Nation-Building 101," 159.

15 Michael Ignatieff, "Human Rights, Power and the State," in *Making States Work*, 66.

16 Fukuyama, "Nation-Building 101," 161.

17 Marina Ottaway, "Nation Building," *Foreign Policy* (September/October 2002), 20.

18 Ibid., 24.

19 Ignatieff, "Human Rights, Power and the State," 71.

20 United Nations Security Council, S/RES/1658(2006), 14 February 2006.

21 "Haiti: Electoral Mirage: A new start proves elusive," *The Economist*, 378, no. 8459 (7–13 January 2006), p. 34.

22 For an examination of the influence of the voodoo religion on Haiti during the Duvalier era, see Elizabeth Abbott, *Haiti: An Insider's History of the Rise and Fall of the Duvaliers* (Montreal: McGraw-Hill, 1988).

23 Paul Farmer, *Pathologies of Power: Health, Human Rights, and the New War on the Poor* (Berkeley: University of California Press, 2005), 236.

The Current and Historical Context

1

The Fall of Aristide and Haiti's Current Predicament

ROBERT FATTON, JR.

To understand Haiti's authoritarian and turbulent politics—only seven of its forty-four presidents have served out their terms, and there have been only two peaceful transitions of power since the beginning of the republic—it is critical to analyze the material and historical circumstances of the colonial period. French colonialism generated an authoritarian tradition rooted in the legacy of the plantation economy. Based on slavery, this economy created a real dilemma for Haiti's founding leaders, a dilemma that was never resolved satisfactorily.

There has always been a very clear link between economic structure and political system in Haiti. For instance, immediately after gaining independence in 1804, the country's founders confronted a cruel choice. They needed to restart a devastated economy and yet the material foundation on which emancipation could flourish was itself inimical to individual freedom. Material recovery depended on agricultural exports—primarily sugar—based on plantation production, which in turn required coercive forms of labour. Haiti's founding fathers, Toussaint, Dessalines, Christophe, and Pétion, were all bent on revitalizing this mode of production, but this posed a crucial dilemma: how to reconcile the safeguard of emancipation and the former slaves' aspirations to become an independent peasantry with the drastic labour discipline required by the plantation economy. If they preserved emancipation by supporting the former slaves' aspirations to become independent peasants, they would ultimately condemn the country to material underdevelopment. If they promoted an immediate economic recovery, Haiti's rulers would be compelled to impose a military-like discipline on the newly freed masses, thereby restricting emancipation itself. Thus, in spite of ending slavery, the Haitian revolution and its subsequent defense reinforced militaristic patterns of behavior and a hierarchical social structure.

Top officers not only gave orders and expected obedience but they reaped the spoils of power. They greatly benefited from the state's grossly unequal redistribution of land, with which they sought to establish themselves as a new class of planters. It is true, however, that the attempt to restore the plantation system was not completely self-serving; it responded also to a question of survival, of generating resources for a strong military to defend Haiti's independence. Haitian rulers had good reasons to fear the aggression of the great powers of the time. As defenders of white supremacy, these powers abhorred the first successful black revolution against slavery and feared the revolution's consequences for their respective empires.

The contradictions of the plantation system, the hostility of western imperial forces, and the class aspirations of Haitian leaders created a historical fissure between a militaristic state of the few and the wider society of the many. In this sense, at the very beginning of independence, a class society was created. There was also the question of colour; mulattos have historically enjoyed more status, privileges, and wealth than the black majority and this reality has generated political tension and conflict between the two groups. The practice of exploiting colour for political ends has always played a major role in Haitian history and continues to reflect the persistence of racial divisions and inequalities inherited from the colonial period.

Haiti's authoritarian tradition is therefore rooted in the legacies of colonial domination and anti-colonial resistance as well as in the vicissitudes of the early period of independence. This tradition, however, is only part of the story. The revolution itself and the struggles of the newly freed slaves to escape the harsh discipline of the plantation economy are clear symbols of the Haitian quest for liberty. In fact, former slaves resisted the attempted restoration of the plantations. They dreamt of agrarian egalitarianism and wanted to own some land, on which they could subsist independently. Thus, emancipation generated the eventual abandonment of the estate economy and the rise of a smallholding peasantry. Haitian rulers were incapable of imposing the rigid discipline required by the plantation system; former slaves could not be easily compelled into a new servitude, having the opportunity to exit the plantation cage and become *marrons*—individuals suspicious of the state and fleeing its authoritarianism. Freedom in this sense implied freedom from any central authority, representative, or otherwise. Thus, the plantation system

gradually collapsed and Haiti became a republic of peasant proprietors relying mostly on subsistence production.

Paradoxically, the rise of this peasantry hindered the limited chance there
might have been for the productive development of the economy. The steady
decline of agriculture was not, however, a simple matter of a peasant economy
of subsistence and of a growing subdivision of land, it was principally the
consequence of the deficiencies of state assistance and the lack of significant
incentives for peasant production. To that extent, peasants have always been
the quintessential *moun andeyo*—those who are taxed but marginalized and
without representation. Not surprisingly, the peasantry's condition has symbolized both the country's material stagnation and acute patterns of class
exploitation.

With rare exceptions, Haiti's numerous constitutions, beginning with the
one promulgated in 1801 under the leadership of Toussaint Louverture have
all ratified the providential authoritarianism of an all-powerful individual.
Toussaint's 1801 Charter set the tone for future generations by declaring him
governor general of the island "for life." While life mandates have not been a
universal feature of all Haitian constitutions, they shaped political customs and
expectations and legitimated the dictatorship of personal rule. In fact, the
overwhelming majority of Haitian rulers have claimed to embody the people
and, indeed, God's will, meaning that they have tended to run the country
like imperial and monarchical presidents. The majority have sought to sup-
press challenges to their supremacy and stifle the autonomous development
of popular forms of power, showing little sympathy for democratic practice.

This authoritarian political tradition is rooted in the material conditions
of the country, reflecting *la politique du ventre*, the "politics of the belly," a
logical consequence of the material scarcity and unproductive economy that
have marked the history of Haiti. Because poverty and destitution had always
been the norm, and private avenues to wealth always rare, politics became an
entrepreneurial vocation, virtually the sole means of material and social
advancement for those not born into wealth and privilege. Controlling the
state turned into a zero-sum game, a violent fight to monopolize the spoils of
political power.

Scarcity has meant that those holding political power have used any means
available to maintain their position of privilege and authority; therefore, relinquishing office peacefully has always been an extremely costly, difficult, and
rare occurrence. Not surprisingly, compromise is uncommon and the army as
the institution with a monopoly of violence has played a decisive role in resolv-
ing and instigating political conflicts.

When François Duvalier's dictatorship came to power in 1957, the army was challenged and undermined by the creation of a paramilitary organization—the *macoutes*. Built to repress dissent and check the army, the macoutes became the vehicle of a despotic order. However, Duvalier had some legitimacy based on a populist and demagogic ideology of *negritude*—a form of black power. Black power in this instance was a cover that masked the ascendancy of a black elite that lorded it over the poor majority. In fact, François Duvalier's regime failed to generate any improvement in Haiti's economic or political life. Moreover, the regime's tyrannical nature caused a massive exodus of Haitians to other shores.

When Duvalier died in 1971, his son Jean-Claude assumed the "Presidency for Life," promising an economic revolution and a political liberalization. In the mid 1970s he launched a relatively "open," technocratic project—what he called *Jean-Claudisme*. He stopped the worst excesses of the macoutes, tolerated some dissent, and rehabilitated the army as an institution. Under these conditions, the country experienced a short period of economic development and hesitant liberalization. By the early 1980s, however, Jean-Claudisme exhausted itself; liberalization was abruptly terminated and repression became the rule again. Moreover, economic growth came to a halt due to massive corruption and state predation.

The liberalization of the late 1970s had contributed to the emergence of an increasingly assertive civil society, however. Many non-governmental organizations challenged the abuses of Duvalierism and began calling for social justice and human rights. Prominent among these organizations was the radical wing of the Catholic Church, known as *Ti Legliz* (little church) which articulated a devastating public critique of *macoutisme* based on the prophetic vision of Liberation Theology. For Ti Legliz and the vast majority of Haitians, real change demanded a massive social, political, and economic transformation, a revolution to overturn almost three decades of Duvalierist domination. It is under these conditions of dissent and growing mass protests that Jean-Claude Duvalier was forced to flee the country in February 1986.

With the collapse of the Duvalier dictatorship, it appeared that the country would start a new history, freed from its long legacy of despotism. A wave of national optimism and euphoria temporarily buried the conflicts among antagonistic actors, institutions, and social classes. It was not long, however, before, these conflicts quickly exploded in a series of confrontations between the army, which had inherited power from the dictator, and an assertive popular movement bent on both *déchouké*—uprooting—Duvalierists and installing a democratic regime. Ultimately, the military resorted to repression, violently aborting the elections of 1987 and organizing farcical ones in 1988, only to seize power again in a coup a few months later.

The army was, however, a profoundly divided institution; internecine struggles soon generated a series of coups and countercoups. Under massive domestic and international pressures, the military leaders were compelled to exit the national palace and facilitate the electoral return of civilians. Led by the charismatic and prophetic messianism of Father Jean-Bertrand Aristide, the huge majority of poor Haitians became *Lavalas*—the flood—an unstoppable flood. Elected in a landslide, Aristide assumed the presidency on 7 February 1991, embodying the hopes and aspirations of the *moun andeyo*.

Aristide was bent on turning the world upside down. He exposed the gigantic class divide separating Haitians, preached that *tout moun se moun*—all human beings are human beings—and advocated extra-parliamentary methods of popular rule. He soon discovered, however, that Haiti's dominant class found this brand of politics to be thoroughly unacceptable. In September 1991, barely seven months after his presidential inauguration, Aristide was overthrown in a bloody coup and forced into exile.

Although incapable of imposing its legitimacy at home or abroad, Raoul Cédras's new military dictatorship remained in power for three violent and repressive years. During this time, Aristide managed to sustain his domestic popularity and mobilize international public opinion against the junta. In September 1994, after a series of failed negotiations between the exiled President and the de facto regime of Cédras, twenty thousand American troops took over Haiti peacefully with the blessing of Aristide as well as the United Nations. Ironically, Aristide, the advocate of liberation theology, the prophet of anti-capitalism, and the nationalist leader, knew that to restore his presidency he had no choice but to depend, and depend utterly, on massive American military assistance.

The circumstances leading to Aristide's "second coming" changed him immensely. Constrained by the overwhelming American presence and by the demands of international financial institutions, he began collaborating with former enemies to implement policies that he had hitherto rejected. He abandoned the priesthood to become a Machiavellian "Prince," maneuvering unsuccessfully to recover the wasted time of exile by prolonging his presidency for three more years. In February 1996, bowing to external pressures, Aristide relinquished the reins of government to his former prime minister, René Préval. However reluctantly he may have done so, Aristide engineered the country's first peaceful electoral transition of power. The rituals of democracy were taking root in spite of manifest shortcomings and flaws.

The Préval presidency was marred by internal power struggles within Lavalas, culminating in a major split between Aristide and his erstwhile supporters. In addition, it symbolized the politics of *doublure*—meaning those holding public office were not those ruling the country. Indeed, secluded in his private residence in Tabarre, Aristide maintained his hegemonic presence; he was the power behind Préval's throne. The result was permanent crisis and political paralysis, the country suffering from increasing corruption, crime, and poverty. The euphoria of 1991 as well as the dreams rekindled by Aristide's return in 1994 gradually faded away, giving rise to popular apathy and cynicism. A series of rigged elections kept democratic rituals alive but undermined the victors' legitimacy. This lack of validation was particularly evident in the controversial 2000 parliamentary and presidential elections, won overwhelmingly by Aristide and his *Fanmi Lavalas* party. Supported by the United States and France, the opposition, regrouped in the *Groupe des 184*, refused to recognize the legality of these ballots, contributing to the second fall of Lavalas and its leader.

Many observers on the left have argued that Aristide's second fall was the result of American imperialism and had little to do with his own policy failures and the country's domestic class structure. While there is a certain plausibility to this argument, it is ultimately flawed; it ignores Haitian agency and exaggerates the omnipotence of US hegemony.

There is no doubt that the Bush administration had little sympathy for Aristide. While it reluctantly acknowledged his legitimacy as president of Haiti, it opposed him for ideological reasons and starved his regime of badly needed foreign assistance. Formulated and exercised by two ultra-conservatives, Roger Noriega and Otto Reich, Washington's policy empowered Aristide's adversaries. The US encouraged and financed the development of the opposition regrouped in *Convergence Démocratique* and the Groupe des 184. Moreover, while it may not have directly supported the rise of the armed insurgency, Washington clearly knew that unsavory elements of the disbanded Haitian army were training in the Dominican Republic with the objective of violently overthrowing Aristide. And yet, it did nothing to stop them. In fact, the US simply abandoned Aristide even though he agreed to the terms of a compromise engineered by the Caribbean Community and Common Market (CARICOM)—a compromise that the opposition rejected. Instead of compelling the opposition to accept it, which would have weakened Aristide's powers and generated a government of national unity, the White House ominously "called into question [Aristide's] fitness to continue to govern" and urged "him to examine his position carefully, to accept responsibility, and to act in the best interests of the people of Haiti" (Office of the Press Secretary, February 28, 2004). In short, once the armed insurgency began and chaos engulfed the country, the Bush administration seized the opportunity to force Aristide's exit.

Imperial America, however, was neither the sole nor necessarily the decisive reason for Aristide's fall, which would have been unlikely had it not been for an armed insurgency and Aristide's own policies. The insurgency, paradoxically, was partly rooted in Aristide's very methods of governance. Aristide did little to transform the inherited authoritarian tradition. Arming young unemployed thugs, the *chimères*, to intimidate the opposition, he sought to govern alone as a messiah and resisted making meaningful concessions. While voicing a radical rhetoric, he followed the neo-liberal scriptures of structural adjustment. In addition, his regime was incapable of resisting the temptations of corruption in spite of its promise of "peace of mind and peace in the belly." Finally, many Lavalas high cadres contributed to the perverse persistence of the "narco-state" (the significant presence of "narco-capitalists") inherited from the military dictatorship.

Not surprisingly, Aristide lost the unconditional popular support he once enjoyed and some of his own chimères turned against him. The assassination of Amiot Metayer, the leader of the Gonaïves' chimères, generated violent anti-Lavalas protests and marked the beginning of the armed insurrection that ultimately forced Aristide into exile. Convinced that it was Aristide himself who ordered Metayer's murder, the "Cannibal Army," led by Metayer's brother Butteur, swore to wage war against the president until he was overthrown. When former soldiers and death squad leaders of the disbanded army joined forces with the Cannibals, Aristide's fate was virtually sealed. The United States and France and, to a lesser degree, Canada gave the final push that led to his fall.

Besieged by the harsh material realities of a devastated economy, his own demons, a reactionary elite, and an increasingly hostile international community, Jean-Bertrand Aristide was incapable of seizing the opportunity to create a mass movement that might have begun to equalize life's chances among Haitians. That the armed insurgents, former members of the disbanded and despised military, found little popular resistance in their march to power, symbolized Aristide's ultimate failure. The triumph of the guns proved once again that the old Creole proverb, *konstitisyon se papye, bayonet se fe*—a constitution is made of paper, but bayonets are made of steel—defined Haitian politics.

The triumph of the gun reflected the proliferation and parcellization of violence. While Lavalas had its chimères, its foes had their own violent means. Disbanded by Aristide in 1994, the army went underground without a clear chain of command, only to resurface with the anti-Aristide insurgency. The army had no monopoly over the means of violence, however. Political groups formed a number of armed gangs over which they had uncertain control. Former macoutes who had joined the Cédras junta's brutal *attachés* and the paramilitary organization Front for the Advancement and Progress of Haiti (FRAPH) re-emerged to form the new death squads and the criminal *Zinglendos* bands and *narcotraficants* established their own violent syndicates. Not surprisingly, the complete breakdown of central authority accompanying the fall of Aristide generated a hellish environment. And yet, Lavalas's successors, the United Nations military contingent (MINUSTAH) and the weak interim government of President Alexandre and Prime Minister Latortue, had neither the will nor the capacity to implement an effective policy of disarmament.

Both the insurgents from the disbanded Haitian army who precipitated Aristide's fall, and the brutal *Chimères* supporting him, have kept their weapons. Under the MINUSTAH-Latortue regime the country and especially Port-au-Prince, endured a climate of insecurity. Gang violence, kidnappings, and political harassment and killings of Aristide's partisans became widespread. This instability coupled with the weak and incompetent electoral commission, led to four postponements of general elections which were finally held on 7 February 2006. While the environment was hardly conducive to free and fair elections, Haitian voters managed to make them so. In spite of major logistical problems and reports of fraud, René Préval was elected president with an overwhelming victory. Receiving more than 51% of the vote in a field of 33 candidates, Préval distanced his closest rival by 40 points.

It is true that a controversial method to count the so-called "blank vote" was devised to allow Préval to obtain the absolute majority and thus avoid a second round. It is also true that this controversial method was engineered only after the fear of generalized chaos materialized when Préval's supporters waged huge popular protests demanding the outright victory of their leader. The fact remains, however, that allegations of fraud amidst the discovery of thousands of burned ballots favouring Préval made it impossible to deny him his victory.

On the other hand, it is very likely that Préval will assume the presidency without a Parliamentary majority. If this happens, he may get embroiled in a major political conflict. Moreover, the social polarization that existed at the time of Aristide's departure has not abated. The deep divide between the urban poor and peasantry who voted massively for Préval and the traditional elites has certainly not disappeared. The two main opponents of Préval, Leslie Manigat and Charles Baker, have hardly accepted their defeat; they are likely to wage an unrelenting fight against the new President. Claiming that Préval's victory was an "electoral coup," and that he is nothing but a stooge of Aristide, they fear that his election will re-establish a new form of Lavalasian power. The post-electoral period is thus likely to be extremely tense and conflictive and the potential for "regime change" will hang like the sword of Damocles over the emerging Préval regime.

These bleak realities have prompted some to advocate for an international protectorate to take temporary control of Haiti for at least ten years. While this idea is not completely farfetched given Haiti's extreme dependence on outside forces, it is unlikely to materialize; and if it did, there is no reason to believe that it would improve the situation of the destitute majority. The past two American occupations of the country contributed neither to long-term self-sustaining economic development nor to lasting democratic forms of accountability. There is little to suggest that, this time around, direct foreign dominance would succeed in ending vicious historical cycles or unleash virtuous ones.

Moreover, the so-called "international community" does not have the appetite for long-term ventures in state-building. The costs are simply too high, especially when one considers that Haiti has no strategic value and no significant natural resources. If the foreign community is really interested in improving conditions in Haiti, it should enter into a long-lasting partnership with a government committed to alleviating poverty. At the moment, however, the record of international financial institutions and the governments they support bode poorly for such an outcome.

The current situation therefore invites pessimism yet the Haitian masses have always struggled against all odds, demonstrating that the possibility of hope is never completely foreclosed. As black slaves, in an age of unfettered white supremacy, they fought for their freedom and defeated the all-powerful French Empire, establishing an independent nation. Currently, fragile networks of community organizations invent means of survival for the poor that defy the ugly realities of squalor and violence. It is these networks that offer an alternative to the existing predicament. They are the embryonic forms of responsive, accountable power. To be truly effective, however, they need the sustained support of a state committed to eradicating the daily squalor facing most Haitians. Given the current balance of forces and the continued power of the affluent minority and international financial organizations, such a convergence of interest remains seriously questionable. The existence of these networks, however, indicates that the possibility of hope is never completely foreclosed. Thus, it is possible to imagine that having been on the brink of a civil war and facing a descent into hell, some key segments of the Haitian political class will finally realize that they should accept the logic of democracy. They may finally come to respect the verdict of the ballot box and understand that they can no longer tolerate the appalling inequalities between the destitute majority and the affluent minority. Perhaps the election of Préval is a sign that the more progressive sectors of society are taking power and that they will have a chance to push forward a modicum of social reforms with the support of Haiti's international partners. If this occurs, then these elections will be meaningful, and then democracy may have a chance. The history of the country and of foreign entanglements in Haiti warns us, however, that material constraints and entrenched class interests weigh heavily against this happy denouement.

Acknowledgement

This is a revised version of a paper presented at The Center for International Governance Innovation (CIGI) and The Canadian Institute for International Affairs (CIIA) on 3 November 2005. Segments of this paper have been previously published as "The Haitian Authoritarian *Habitus* and the Contradictory Legacy of 1804," *Journal of Haitian Studies* 10, no. 1 (2004): 22–43.

2

Assisting a Neighbour
Haiti's Challenge to North American Policy-Makers

ROBERT MAGUIRE

Assisting Haiti: An American Allegory

One day, while at his ranch in Texas, US President George W. Bush was engaged in a trademark vacation activity: clearing brush. Suddenly, Mr. Bush happened upon a genie's lamp. Immediately, he rubbed it. When the genie appeared, he told the President that he had only one wish, not the standard three wishes. After all, Mr. Bush was the leader of the world's most powerful nation, wasn't he—why would he need more than one? In response, the president pulled a map from his shirt pocket and gave it to the genie, exclaiming, "Oh good! Use your powers to solve the problems I'm facing in this place." The genie examined the map, which was of Iraq, and handed it back to the perspiring president, remarking, "Well…I'm good, but I'm not *that* good. How about something else?" Whereupon, Mr. Bush pulled a folded-up paper from his other shirt pocket and handed it to the genie, adding, "OK, maybe you can solve this one." As the genie unfolded the paper he saw written at its top: "Haiti." Beneath that heading, he saw a long list of items, which he began to read. Before even reaching halfway down the list, however, the genie let out a sigh, rolled his eyes, shook his head, and handed the paper back to the American president, pleading, "Please sir, may I see that first map again?"

Involvement in Haiti

Mr. Bush is hardly the first leader in North America to become involved with Haiti and to be troubled by conditions there. His earliest predecessors,

US presidents going back more than two hundred years, were preoccupied with the Caribbean country. Following Haiti's independence in 1804, Washington viewed the country as a threat to US national security interests, and imposed policies of political and economic isolation. Southern slave owners viewed the former French colony's "virus of freedom" as a disease that could potentially spread to their plantations.

With emancipation in the US in 1862, that threat disappeared, but the Black republic off its southern shores did not. The United States continued to view Haiti with suspicion and distrust and, as it evolved into a hemispheric power, a domain in which its interests could be imposed. In the late-nineteenth and early-twentieth centuries, US policies tended toward what might be characterized as "bullyism," with repeated episodes of gunboat diplomacy and military incursion. Haiti's occupation by US Marines from 1915 to 1934 followed. Although the occupying forces achieved significant progress in building Haiti's infrastructure they did not undertake reforms to address political, economic and social disequilibrium within the country. Indeed, Washington's favouritism toward the country's mulatto elites during the occupation exacerbated social, economic, and political cleavages within the country.

Unilateral military approaches aimed at improving conditions in Haiti gradually evolved to become somewhat kinder and gentler later in the century. This is not to say that political adventurism toward Haiti disappeared following the occupation, but rather that involvement expanded in the second half of the twentieth century to include significant investment in bilateral and multilateral foreign aid projects, and interventions by hundreds of private voluntary, humanitarian, and non-governmental organizations.

Involvement also expanded during the past fifty years to include Canada's participation in Haiti initiatives, along with the engagement of multilateral actors such as the United Nations and its constellation of organizations, the Organization of American States (OAS), and the multilateral development banks. Both the United States and Canada promoted this multilateral engagement, and then supported it with financial and human resources. Since 1995, and particularly in the past two years, the United States and Canada have collaborated closely in their support of, and involvement with, UN Security Council-sanctioned military intervention and peacekeeping operations in Haiti.

More recently, North American involvement has evolved to include participation of the Haitian Diaspora living in both the United States and Canada, as Carlo Dade outlines in greater detail in chapter six. That participation has included cash remittances and other resources provided by the Diaspora to family left behind, to the tune of an estimated US$1 billion annually. Increasingly, professionally and economically successful Haitians living overseas are involved in their homeland through charitable interventions, such as medical missions, and through direct economic investment. It is important to note that the Diaspora also promotes its interests in Haiti by informing and influencing its adopted country's policies toward the Caribbean homeland. This is especially noticeable in Florida and Quebec, where concentrations of voters with Haitian backgrounds have played significant roles in electing officials with a special interest in keeping Haiti on the US and Canadian national agendas. The efforts of the Maryland-based National Organization for the Advancement of Haitians (NOAH) stand out as a choice example of successful Haitian immigrants pooling their resources to impact policy. Increasingly, the Haitian Diaspora is also involved directly in Haitian politics, particularly as financiers and appointed officials, and is attempting to gain voting and political candidacy rights in its native land.

Haiti has been the beneficiary of significant North American and other international human and financial resources aimed at improving conditions there, especially over the past fifty years. This was particularly true between 1994 and 1999, following the first UN-sanctioned intervention and peacekeeping mission, and the series of UN technical support missions that followed. However, it is common to hear lamentations that conditions in Haiti have not improved—that they are, in fact, deteriorating—despite the expenditures of billions of dollars. An overview of those conditions and the challenges they present will set the stage for a brief examination of how such lamentations might be addressed.

Challenges

If there really had been a list for Mr. Bush to give a genie, it might have included the following list of challenges confronting policy-makers: geographic proximity, economic and environmental deterioration, political and social conflict, and public safety deficiencies. Geographic proximity is particularly relevant to the United States and some of Haiti's other immediate neighbours.

Geographic proximity A glance at a map of the Caribbean shows Haiti's position in the western hemisphere and its proximity to the United States. By air, the Caribbean country is only about an hour and a half from Miami and Haiti's proximity to Florida has been a major reason for Washington's involvement. One could surmise that had the country been further from US shores, located, say, in the general area of the Falkland Islands, US involvement would be practically nil. But that, of course, is not the case.

Haiti's proximity to the United States has given rise to two particular challenges, each helping to fuel and sustain US involvement in recent decades. The first is migration. The spectre of mass, unregulated migration of Haitians traveling by boat to Florida's shores has sent shivers down the spines of US policy-makers since the late 1970s, when "boatpeople" from Haiti first began to appear in significant numbers on Florida beaches. The southern state is so close to Haiti that this voyage can occur without intermediate stops. At the same time, it can include transit landings in the Bahamas, or, for those boats seriously off course, in Cuba. More recently, an alternate route has been established whereby Haitians, having crossed into the Dominican Republic, are transported by air to the eastern Caribbean island of Dominica. From there they are smuggled by sailboat to the US Virgin Islands. Five thousand Haitians are estimated to have entered Dominica during the first nine months of 2005. Although illegal, mass migration of Haitians is a US concern, but it also concerns a number of the Caribbean country's neighbours.

In response to the tens of thousands of Haitians fleeing their country's political turmoil, poverty, and environmental degradation, successive American administrations have enacted controversial policies that view Haitians principally as unwanted economic migrants, interdicting them when possible on the high seas and, as a rule, returning them to Haiti. The current Bush administration has cited the successful arrival by boat of undocumented Haitians on Florida's beaches as an example of how international terrorists might arrive in the United States. This supposition has provided an additional rationale for strictly enforced interdiction and return policies aimed at Haitian refugees.

The migration issue and related policies generate considerable anxiety among the more than 250,000 Haitians residing in the politically high-stakes state of Florida, as well as among Haitians elsewhere in the United States. This adds an important domestic political dynamic to the issue, and to US policies toward Haiti. Estimates of the Haitian Diaspora in the United States run as high as one million. The Haitian migration issue has also galvanized the attention of other high-profile US political constituencies, most notably the Congressional Black Caucus (CBC) in the US House of Representatives.

The second geographically linked challenge is Haiti's location as a conduit for trafficking cocaine into the United States, sometimes by way of the Dominican Republic and Puerto Rico. A Caribbean Basin map reveals Haiti's strategic location between a principal hemispheric narcotics producer and exporter—Colombia—and North American consumers. The US government estimates that somewhere around 10 per cent of cocaine consumed annually by Americans passes through Haiti. Like migration, drug trafficking has contributed to casting Haiti as an international and a domestic political issue in the United States.

While Haiti's role as a drug transshipment point is of particular concern to the United States, like migration, this problem concerns some of Haiti's neighbours as well. This is particularly true of the Dominican Republic, through which significant quantities of cocaine arriving in Haiti are transshipped prior to reaching the United States. Despite its less proximate location to Haiti, Canada also has "a dog in this fight," since some of the South American product moved through Haiti also slips into Canada.

Drug trafficking is also having a debilitating and destabilizing impact in Haiti itself. Much of the unrest verging on anarchy that plagues that country today is attributed to deleterious effects of the drug trade such as gang violence, political corruption, and weapons trafficking. Complaints have been made by Haitian officials that Haitian nationals repatriated by the United States and Canada following criminal convictions become actors in drug trafficking, criminal, and politically affiliated gangs, thus adding to the country's unrest. However, their complaints have been ignored. This repatriation of convicted criminals adds a dangerous transnational character to the drug trafficking issue.

Economic and Environmental That Haiti, as the Western Hemisphere's least developed nation, is mired in widespread, severe poverty is undeniable. That its severe poverty presents major challenges to those who wish to assist it is equally beyond doubt. Over the past three decades, since the February 1986 ouster of the Duvalier family dictatorship opened prospects for Haiti to chart a new political, social and economic course, little sustained progress has been made in addressing its economic woes. Indeed, since the 1990s, the country's economy has deteriorated, shrinking at an annual estimated rate of 0.4 per cent. Over that same period, Haiti has experienced negative per capita Gross Domestic Product (GDP) growth, while its man-made infrastructure and natural environment have continued to deteriorate significantly. Deforestation, erosion, and pollution of both fresh and salt water resources have brought the country to the brink of environmental collapse. Production of essential domestic food crops such as rice and corn, and of export crops such as mangoes and coffee, is virtually stagnant as the country's infrastructure deteriorates, its natural resource base erodes, and investment in agriculture, farmers, and restoring the environment is virtually non-existent.

Successive Haitian governments have failed to improve the country's human resource capacity, and both external investors and Haitians with the resources to invest are discouraged by the deteriorating infrastructure, political instability and corruption, as well as dangers of doing business in a country where uncertainty and violence reign and where impunity from the rule of law is rampant. As a result, as much as 70 per cent of Haiti's working-age population has no regular employment. Although Haiti's per capita GDP is variously estimated at somewhere in the range of $400, more than half of the country's population struggles to make ends meet on less than one dollar a day. And, Haiti's population of approximately eight million, 40 per cent of whom are younger than fifteen years of age, is growing at an annual rate of 1.8 per cent. This means that in the span of thirty-nine years the population will double. Only the kindness of strangers who bring aid to the country, and of extended family members who send home money and other resources, keeps the country afloat. The aforementioned cash transfers from Haitians living overseas play an especially critical role in enabling those left behind to afford life's necessities, including education, housing, and health.

Political and Social At the root of this dismal picture of virtually unbridled emigration, drug trafficking, widespread severe poverty, economic decay, and environmental degradation are challenges that arise as a result of the country's dysfunctional political system and deep polarization among its citizens. The political system has been characterized largely by strong man rule and by "winner-takes-all" politics. The flip side of this winner-takes-all system is that "losers undermine winners," resulting in a volatile mix of constant political violence and confrontation. To ensure their longevity, leaders ally themselves with the country's security apparatus—be it the army, paramilitary forces, or political gangs—and with its economic elites. The well-known Haitian proverb "Constitutions are made of paper, whereas bayonets are made of steel" is emblematic of both the high-stakes struggle for political authority and the dubious status of rule of law in the country.

Haiti has been widely characterized as a state that preys on its people. Leaders and elites have ensured that the predatory state serves their interests, with little regard for the well-being of others in society. Little interest has been exhibited in human resource investment or in the development of the countryside, where the majority of Haiti's citizens reside, save for what must be done to ensure that they can extract resources and maintain control. Indeed, in the last fifty years, the only systematic presence of the state in rural settlements scattered throughout the country were the income tax office and the army outpost: one to siphon off resources and the other to ensure the job was done.

As a result of this predatory system, there has been neither a social safety net for the vast majority of Haiti's citizens nor a functional social contract between those who govern and those who are governed. For example, one meets farmers who have tilled the soil for decades without ever encountering a government agronomist. The vast majority of the country's one thousand or so state agronomists rarely leave the environs of the country's capital, Port-au-Prince, where no one farms. Without significant annual public investment in essential services such as education, health care, and potable water, it is not surprising that few public schools, health care facilities, and water systems are in evidence and that what exists of these services has become the domain of non-state actors. The national doctor to patient ratio is 1: 4,000. Haiti's life expectancy averages 49.1 years, and more than 50 per cent of the population is undernourished.

Adding to Haiti's political challenges are those presented by the society's deeply engrained polarization. Haiti has been characterized as an example of apartheid in the Caribbean, where unbridgeable divisions based on class, ethnicity, race, and even geographic location result in the systematic exclusion of vast numbers of citizens from playing a meaningful role in their country's social, economic, and political life. In Creole, these excluded or marginalized ones are sometimes referred to as the *moun andeyo*, or the people on the outside. Including both the rural and urban poor, they comprise some 75 per cent or more of the population. Conversely, the country's polarization has resulted in a small group of economic insiders—sometimes identified as 1 per cent of the population—dominating the country's economy and controlling at least half of its GDP.

Public Safety Haiti's challenges and deficiencies in public safety stem largely from the fact that the institution traditionally responsible for this matter—the army—served as a mechanism to enforce the predatory state system. Rather than protecting the national integrity of Haiti, the country's army preyed on and repressed Haiti's more vulnerable citizens, and for decades was deeply involved in drug trafficking and other corrupt practices. Throughout the twentieth century, it served principally as a force to fight the Haitian people. In 1995, President Aristide disbanded the army, preserving only a military band to fulfill a constitutional mandate that Haiti have an army. Subsequently, public security responsibility was given to a fledgling national police force, the Haitian National Police (HNP). Ultimately, that force has proven unequal to the task of improving Haiti's public safety environment. Corruption, abuse of power and authority, the untimely withdrawal of crucial international support, and political manipulation all have conspired to demoralize the HNP, making it as much a part of the problem as the solution.

Adding to challenges presented by this institutional disarray is the dysfunctional nature of Haiti's judicial and penal systems. Justice is plagued by impunity, corruption, political manipulation, and favouritism. The prison system is a dark recess prone to abuse. Layered on top of these institutional deficiencies that plague prospects for public safety is the presence of the aforementioned criminal and political gangs, the rampant spread of small arms to diverse groups of "spoilers," and current efforts to resurrect the discredited army.

In all, Haiti presents to US and Canadian policy-makers the challenge of a highly polarized and demoralized society with a tendency toward both strong-arm politics and one-man rule, as well as intense competition to gain or protect social, economic, and political privilege. Weak and dysfunctional public institutions, rampant drug trafficking, gang violence and criminal impunity, extreme poverty, deeply engrained polarization, and environmental degradation—all are ingredients in a recipe for social, political, and economic collapse. It is no wonder, then, that despite considerable allocation of external human and financial resources to address these challenges, Haiti remains a country on the verge of failure, and no wonder that our allegorical genie chose Iraq over Haiti.

Shortening the Genie's List

How might policy-makers improve conditions in Haiti today? This question is all the more important given that, following the second UN-sanctioned military intervention in a decade, US, Canadian, and other international actors are hinting that this may be the last chance for improving conditions before the country completely collapses. It might be helpful to consider some of the obstacles that seem to have thwarted previous efforts to improve conditions in the troubled Caribbean country, particularly within the past decade.

The principal factor undermining external efforts over the past decade to transform Haiti into a stable, functioning, inclusive, and modern democratic state that serves all its citizens, has been the tendency to seek a quick exit. Policy-makers today must resist the temptation to intervene only when a crisis reaches the boiling point, stabilize the country, hold an election, and then drastically reduce their presence and engagement. In a world with so many crises, it may be true that sustaining the international community's interest in a country as small as Haiti is tough—particularly when it has been so difficult to achieve and maintain success there and when "Haiti fatigue" has emerged among many international players. For the United States and Canada, however, Haiti's proximity, the growing presence and influence of their Haitian Diaspora populations, and the Caribbean country's importance as both an international and domestic political issue compel not only sustained engagement, but also sustained leadership in keeping others engaged.

Sustained engagement and leadership alone, however, will not shorten the genie's list. In addition to struggling against the tendency to seek a quick exit, US, Canadian and other policy-makers must also address other issues that are difficult by themselves and have been compounded by this quick exit tendency.

They must avoid politically driven decisions that result in quick fix approaches and departure deadlines incompatible with the requirements for enduring reform in a society as troubled as Haiti. Institution-building in such a fragile state requires significant resources applied over extended periods. They should also pay adequate and equal attention to all three pillars of public safety reform: police, judiciary, and prisons. Prior efforts focused heavily on the police, but left the other two pillars largely unreformed. This sabotaged efforts by the newly formed police force to improve public safety, fuelling latent tendencies of corruption and unauthorized use of force among uniformed personnel. It also left unaddressed the serious problem of impunity. The deterioration of the HNP and the rise of gang and other criminal violence was the result.

It is important that policy-makers ensure that there are sufficient and consistent resource flows, particularly in support of public institutions and state reform. Initially robust infusions of assistance that dwindle before the job is done will lead to erosion of gains or "backsliding." Significantly, as the fledgling HNP began to run into trouble, international actors, led by the United States, disengaged by withholding funds, making an already dangerous situation even worse. Another grave problem was the refusal by external actors to support state institutions—leaving them lacking capacity, woefully incompetent, and even more prone to corruption—while conversely focusing aid on non-state actors. As seen by developments in the early 2000s, this is a recipe for frustration, lack of sustainability, and, ultimately, disaster. Non-governmental organizations (NGOs) have a role to play but, fundamentally, in weak states such as Haiti it is the institutions of the state that must be strengthened in order to play their legitimate roles in serving citizens. Even if forced to hold one's nose, it is much wiser to engage the state (particularly if its leaders are democratically elected)—by supporting it while maintaining leverage over it—than to isolate the state, leaving it further weakened and the society in greater danger of chaos. This should be one of the most important lessons emanating from recent experience in Haiti.

Policy-makers must seek to eliminate divergent priorities originating from different capitals, and between and within governments or international organizations. A decade ago, the involvement in Haiti of one major player—the United States—was guided by an anti-nation-building/no mission creep ethos that emanated in large part from experience not relevant to Haiti. Specifically, that experience was the Black Hawk Down episode in Somalia, where, after the focus changes from delivering food supplies to nation-building, a number of violent battles ensued that killed American soldiers and Somali militia and citizens. Policy-makers must resist both generalizing from one context to the next and applying the "one size fits all" approach to highly particular situations. The ethos of staying focused on the mission and not engaging in nation-building had the result a decade ago of limiting program flexibility within Haiti and also the crucial support needed for sustained international involvement. Additionally, within Washington, partisan political squabbles resulted in withheld or withdrawn financial support of international efforts. From 2001 to 2004 in particular, mixed or competing messages from Washington exacerbated political conflict and violence in Haiti, undermining internationally backed attempts to seek peaceful resolutions to differences among political, economic and social sectors within the deeply polarized country.[1]

It is essential to provide sufficient, sustained attention to imperatives for economic growth and humanitarian progress, particularly those related to social conflict and poverty reduction. Military responses alone do not provide solutions to these issues. Rather, economic growth, poverty reduction, and humanitarian relief programs must attract the "buy-in" and participation of all sectors of Haitian society. This must be achieved through dialogue and reconciliation with the benefits accruing to those most in need. Further, quick fix programs that fail to address the root causes of poverty and inequality, or that cannot sustain immediate results, will build resentment and desperation among Haiti's poor—the *moun andeyo*—and will lead to continued, perhaps even increased, tension, conflict, violence, and the desire to escape through dangerous and illegal migration. It is particularly important that initiatives to expand opportunities for social and economic mobility among Haiti's poor be undertaken—but not at the expense of participation and inclusion. Factory jobs at low wages may help to address issues of unemployment and may infuse some needed resources into poor households, albeit insufficient for anything more than immediate survival. However, these jobs do not offer much prospect for mobility. Investment in Haiti's productive base, particularly the restoration of its environment and improved prospects for domestic and export agricultural production, will directly benefit tens, if not hundreds, of thousands of poor Haitian families in rural areas. Moreover, this form of investment will also indirectly benefit those living in Haiti's increasingly stressed cities.

Policy-makers should be prepared to confront and abate Haiti's complex social, economic, and political dichotomization, and the insecurity and volatility it brings to society. The "fear factor" among Haitians isolated from each other is catastrophically high. International players must engage forcefully and deftly in diffusing that factor and the resultant polarization and violence. This process must take place in Washington and Ottawa as much as it must occur in Port-au-Prince. Indeed, in recent years, Haiti's debilitating polarity has flowed into North America's cities and into the headquarters of international organizations worldwide, influencing actors there to take sides, thereby undermining decision-making process and policies. It is of crucial importance that international actors not take sides in Haiti, but rather, that they promote and achieve dialogue and reconciliation among Haiti's conflictive factions. Effective peacekeeping cannot be undertaken in the absence of peacemaking among Haiti's conflictive social, economic and political factions. Thus far, however, peacemaking has not been achieved. Peacekeepers have been sent to Haiti in the absence of a framework for peace to guide them and Haiti's conflictive parties. This has placed everyone involved in Haiti—UN Peacekeepers, the civilian actors who work in their footsteps, and the people of Haiti—at a great disadvantage.

In their quest to assist Haiti, North American policy-makers have many difficult and persistent challenges to face. Sadly, there will be no genie in the lamp to help them to magically overcome them. But with a realistic and objective understanding and assessment of Haiti and its challenges, and a purposeful focus on lessons learned from prior attempts to address them, there is still hope that Haiti can be nudged back from the precipice of collapse and become a positive presence in the Americas.

Note

1 This issue is the focus of a recent journalistic investigative report, Walt Bogdanich and Jenny Nordberg, "Democracy Undone: Mixed US Signals Helped Tilt Haiti toward Chaos," *New York Times,* 29 January 2006.

3

The Economic Dimension of Peacebuilding in Haiti
Drawing on the Past to Reflect on the Present

YASMINE SHAMSIE

Haiti is a country that has frustrated donor governments and agencies, at times to the point of disengagement. One of the more daunting objectives pursued by outside actors has been poverty reduction. As the peacebuilding literature indicates, and as donors recognize, poverty is among the factors leading to violence, insecurity, and political instability, making its reduction crucial to long-term peace, development, and democratic governance.

This chapter examines the economic development model that has been charted for Haiti by outside actors since 1994, and assesses whether it is likely to reduce poverty and address the vast imbalance between rich and poor. I argue that while the model advanced by donors and international financial institutions (IFIs) may help reactivate the Haitian economy, it is not clear that it will lead to a reduction in poverty. There are two reasons for this. First, the economic development model places a great deal of faith in the development of Haiti's export potential—more specifically export assembly manufacturing for the US market. The problem with this strategy is that it has already been tried and has failed to reduce poverty levels. Also envisaged as part of the current development strategy are policies aimed at harnessing the potential of the private sector, viewed as the engine of economic growth. While support for these activities can indeed lead to growth in certain economic sectors, I will present some caveats to relying on them as instruments of poverty reduction. There is another reason why this development model is unlikely to seriously affect poverty levels; it devotes little attention to Haiti's rural sector, where the poorest people live and work.

The chapter begins with an assessment of the first attempt at economic development via export processing zones, focusing on the strategy's impact on poverty levels and inequality. This is followed by an examination and assessment of current development plans.

Export Processing Zones in Haiti: Taking Stock[1]

Haiti is the poorest country in the region. Its Gross Domestic Product (GDP) per capita is less than half that of Bolivia, which sits one rung above it as the second poorest country in the hemisphere. According to a recent study, "56 per cent of [Haiti's] population live on less than one dollar per day, compared to less than 25 per cent in all other countries of the region except Nicaragua and El Salvador. Poverty is deeper and more pervasive than in the rest of Latin America."[2] Haiti's rural areas and its peasant farmers are without doubt the most destitute. The rural poor account for three-quarters of the country's poor, with only one quarter of these having access to safe water and one in six to basic sanitation.[3] Haiti is also the most unequal country in the region, with the starkest division between rich and poor. In order to explore the potential of the export assembly sector as a tool to reduce poverty levels, this section briefly summarizes Haiti's development experience during the 1970s and '80s, when export manufacturing was at its peak in terms of investment levels and employment.

As noted earlier, the export development manufacturing model is not new to Haiti. It was initiated as far back as the 1950s and '60s and eagerly expanded during the 1970s and '80s. The first generation of US firms, which established their operations during the 1950s under the dictatorship of François "Papa Doc" Duvalier (1957–71), failed to spark development, due, for the most part, to the lack of infrastructure, local capital, and basic services. In other words, the strategy itself was not discredited. Consequently, when Jean-Claude "Baby Doc" Duvalier came to power, his regime expanded the country's export manufacturing industry with particular emphasis on the assembly industry.

Incentives offered to attract US industries to the country during Jean-Claude Duvalier's regime were generous. Corporations were offered a tax holiday of ten years, complete profit repatriation, and a guaranteed non-unionized work force. These incentives proved to be quite effective and led to the massive expansion of assembly operations. Whereas primary commodities had constituted 100 per cent of Haitian exports in 1960, they accounted for only 61 per cent of the total by 1979.[4] Exports from light industry grew at an average annual rate of 40 per cent during the seventies, with the number of companies engaged in assembly operations increasing from thirteen in 1966 to 154 by 1981.[5] By the early 1980s, Haiti was second only to Mexico among the US subcontracting territories in the western hemisphere, having attracted some 240 multinational corporations employing sixty thousand workers (mostly women).[6] In fact, in 1985, one year before Jean-Claude Duvalier's forced exile, Haiti ranked ninth in the world in the assembly of goods for US consumption, with this sub-sector generating more than half the country's industrial exports and earning one-quarter of its foreign exchange.[7]

The US was the most important bilateral donor in Haiti and its aid programs during this period actively supported the restructuring of the Haitian economy, and more specifically the establishment of export processing zones. Assistance was directed toward the country's infrastructure and technical-administrative apparatus since these were crucial to the assembly sector's success. The level of US aid to Haiti increased every year in the early 1970s, and fourfold between 1975 and 1976. It is important to note that, as export processing was being encouraged, peasant agriculture was being discouraged. The United States Agency for International Development (USAID) employed a number of strategies, including dumping massive amounts of rice on the Haitian market, thereby undercutting peasant producers, in order to encourage the shift from subsistence agriculture to agricultural export production.[8]

It is clear that there was a tremendous expansion of the export processing industry during Jean-Claude Duvalier's regime. The effects of this trend were multifarious but mainly disappointing, most significantly on the poverty front. The light industry/subcontracting strategy was expected to help put Haiti's fiscal house in order; however, this anticipated benefit never materialized. Haiti's debt increased from US$53 million in 1973 to US$366 million in 1980, double the growth rate of external indebtedness in the region as a whole over that same period.[9] By 1981, foreign-exchange reserves were exhausted. The country's balance of payments also suffered, forcing even the World Bank to concede that the assembly industry had made "almost no fiscal contribution" to the economy.[10]

The assembly industry also contributed to the country's trade deficit which rose from US$12.4 million in 1970 to US$68.4 million in 1975 and US$183 million in 1980.[11] Compounding the country's fiscal problems was the fact that the presence of the assembly industry allowed an increasing quantity of imports to escape customs controls. In a country like Haiti, where most of the government's resources come from customs duties, this constituted a grave problem. All classes of luxury goods entered the country free of taxes on the pretext that they were essential to the firms operating in the Haiti's industrial park. Statistics, which are generally considered to be on the forgiving side, reveal that, between 1970 and 1976, the value of merchandise that entered untaxed rose from US$11.4 million to US$112.2 million.

These developments had significant repercussions for Haiti's poorest citizens. Faced with the consequent shortfall in revenues from imports, the government predictably turned to internal taxes to compensate for losses at the customs-houses. (In the case of Haiti, internal taxes did not consist of income taxes or taxes on private sector activity; they were mainly consumption taxes.) From 1980 to 1984, total government revenues increased from US$134.4 million to US$189.9 million. In those same years, custom revenues declined from US$65 million to less than US$57 million, even though import quantities and values continued to rise. The increase in government income, therefore, was due solely to an increase in internal revenues, which jumped from US$69.3 million in 1980 to US$132 million in 1984.[12] The shift to internal taxes (local market and consumer taxes) adversely affected peasants and the urban lower classes in particular, meaning that the poorest were most harshly impacted, which had repercussions for poverty and inequality levels.

This development strategy also contributed to drastic increases in the cost of food and housing, again with adverse effects on the poorest. Food prices soared because of a rural exodus, as both agricultural production and food distribution workers were lured to Port-au-Prince's manufacturing sector by the promise of better wages. It is worth noting that women, the assembly industry's target labour force, were also the mainstay of the country's marketing system for locally grown produce.[13] While no systematic correlation has been established between the needs of the assembly industry for female labour and decreasing levels of food production and food distribution, the relation between the two is certainly not far-fetched, particularly given that wages in the Delmas industrial park were ten times what a peasant would have earned.[14]

As local food production diminished, imported foodstuffs flooded the country, with the value of imported food rising from US$10.7 million in 1970 to US$62.1 million in 1976. Seven years after Jean-Claude Duvalier came to power and promoted his export-processing zone strategy, one-fifth of Haitian imports were foodstuffs, costing the country US$89 million. As Trouillot notes, "as the volume and price of imported food rose, so did the price of locally produced food, which was now available in smaller quantities and more heavily taxed. Thus the average price of all foodstuffs more than doubled between 1975 and 1985, with such common items as sweet potatoes leading the increase."[15] It should not be surprising that the first demonstrations aimed at toppling the dictatorship were food riots.

Before too long, Haiti was no longer able to make payments on its loans. In order to assist the Haitian government in meeting its financial obligations, the United States Agency for International Development (USAID) and the World Bank designed a revised development strategy that, once again, centred on the export of agro-industrial and assembly products. The plan for the agro-industrial sector entailed the planting of coffee and cocoa on marginal hillside lands and reorienting production on flat and productive lands toward fruit and vegetables for the US winter market or toward industrial processing for export. The development of these new agro-industries implied shifting 30 per cent of all cultivated land from the production of food for local consumption (affecting food security) to the production of export crops.[16] The assembly industry would be given a boost through new trade regulations, tax holidays, credit funds, and technical assistance projects.

Despite this added impetus and stimulus from international donors, the strategy failed to bring about the expected economic benefits or a reduction in poverty levels. In fact, poverty and income concentration increased during the years that the model was employed in great part because it favoured the economic development of Port-au-Prince (the urban sector) over the rest of the country (the rural sector). The rapid spread of these urban-based industries served to reinforce an already worrisome economic polarization in Haiti. In short, the gap between rich and poor widened as urbanization increased. Trouillot illustrates this tendency with developments in the electricity sector, noting that while the production of electricity increased, only certain social sectors benefited, with Port-au-Prince and its surrounding boroughs consuming 93 per cent of the electricity produced in the country in 1979.[17]

The increased polarization was so obvious that by the early 1980s even the World Bank—a strong supporter of the assembly industry—suggested that factories should be interspersed throughout the country rather than concentrated in the Delmas industrial park, located on the edge of Port-au-Prince. Few backward linkages to the Haitian economy were created under this plan and workers' wages actually decreased, so that in 1980 they were worth less than they had been in 1970.

As noted at the outset, the main reason the light industry formula failed to reduce poverty was that it avoided addressing problems associated with rural Haiti. However, ignoring the peasantry has been the norm in Haiti, with the rural population having been traditionally cut off from the national government and development policy formulation. According to much of the literature, national politics have been conducted "almost without reference to the aspirations of the rural masses."[18] For instance, in 1986, agriculture accounted for 35 per cent of national production and 66 per cent of the economically active population were engaged in this sector. Still, between 1970 and 1985 the problems of the rural communities were not only ignored, they were aggravated.[19]

Mark Weisbrot argues that, all in all, the assembly industry did little to generate employment, growth, and economic development. His examination reveals a dismal balance sheet:

> In 1990 (the last year of normal economic activity before the coup and embargo), 84 per cent of this sector's exports were composed of imported inputs. When one takes into account that much of the profits are taken out of the country, the net contribution of this sector to Haiti's foreign exchange earnings is negligible…It is well recognized that this sector contributes relatively little to employment: at its peak it employed 60,000 workers, which dropped to 4,000 after the coup; it has since grown to about 18,000. Nor does it contribute to backward and forward linkages that might develop other sectors of the economy. So the only selling point of this sector is that it supposedly provides exports that can fuel the growth of the economy; however, this is a statistical misrepresentation based on counting the whole value of this sector's exports as though it were produced in Haiti, when only a small fraction of it actually is.[20]

According to Haitian social scientist Suzy Castor, author of this book's conclusion, a similar picture appears when one examines the earlier capitalist enclaves established as far back as the 1920s and in the immediate post-World War II period. Haiti's assembly industries never became sufficiently developed to have a real impact on the overall economy, let alone Haitian society. This, according to Castor, was largely because the industry employed "an accumulation model based on super-exploitation of labour (very low salaries, no social security, prohibition of bargaining rights etc.)."[21] Although the strategy accomplished little in economic and social terms, it continues to appeal to international donors.

Economic Development Plans Post-1994

In mid-October 1994, just prior to the re-establishment of constitutional rule, the Inter-American Development Bank took the lead role in a Joint Assessment Mission to determine how to best address Haiti's economic and social problems.[22] The product of that mission was the Emergency Economic Recovery Program (EERP)—a blueprint for the economic and social reconstruction of Haiti. The EERP was followed in 1996 by a long-term US$1.2 billion-dollar development and reconstruction plan. More recently, in 2004, donors advanced a new short-term plan, the Interim Cooperation Framework (ICF). In accordance with conventional economic thinking, each of these plans places a strong emphasis on the reactivation of export-manufacturing and little emphasis on the rural sector.

The first plan, the EERP, was designed to establish a stable macroeconomic environment and to provide an incentive framework for private sector investment. Peasant producers in the countryside received little direct aid from this short-term plan. In a nation where almost 65 per cent of the population is engaged in some form of agricultural production, assisting peasant farmers would have been the most direct way of alleviating poverty and addressing the vast imbalance between rich and poor. Despite this, international donors did very little to augment peasant access to productive resources.[23] As one observer notes: "Indeed, direct investments in peasant agriculture accounted for *less than one percent* of the US$550 million in donor aid and loans distributed in FY 94/95" (emphasis added).[24] The following fiscal year, there was a marginal increase in funds targeted to agriculture, but those funds were aimed at road and irrigation system repair and at promoting export crops such as coffee and mangoes (rather than foodstuffs such as oils, meat, and beans). While repairing the country's roads was a worthy goal, and did assist some farmers in transporting their goods to market, it did not affect the great majority of peasant producers (mostly women) who head-load their produce to market or transport it on donkeys. The provision of seeds, tools, fertilizer, credit, and marketing co-operatives would have been of greater benefit to those in the countryside.

It is also worth noting that the policy framework paper developed by the International Monetary Fund (IMF), in collaboration with the World Bank and Haiti's ministry of finance, was very specific in its instructions to the Haitian government regarding credit. While the state could implement policies that would enable others to establish credit funds, the government was instructed not to provide funds for agricultural research, training, or productive credit to the poor.[25] Moreover, donors understood that advocating the liberalization of Haiti's markets, and more specifically the lowering of protective tariffs on rice, the country's most basic staple, would devastate Haitian producers. As far back as 1987, authors of a USAID report warned that these policies would probably bring a loss of income to rice-growing peasants of about US$15 million a year, further reducing their already poor standard of living. Almost ten years later, in 1995, another report was commissioned which concluded, once again, that tariff reductions of between 3 and 10 per cent advocated by IFIS would threaten the very existence of the Haitian rice farmer.[26]

The current aid and development plan for Haiti, the 2004 ICF, aims, like all plans before it, to create the conditions necessary for reducing poverty. It advances a number of policy goals to achieve this: strengthening the private sector, harnessing the potential of the informal sector and the Diaspora, encouraging rural development, and resurrecting the export manufacturing (assembly) sector.

Support for the Haitian private sector and entrepreneurship in general could prove to be a valuable strategy for combating poverty. At the same time, it would be overly optimistic to presume that the poorest Haitians, many of whom make their living in the informal sector or in rural areas, would inevitably benefit from a more robust formal private sector. There is little data to support this assumption. As Brian Tomlinson points out, even the staunchest supporter of private sector development, the World Bank, notes in a recent multiple-country study "that the evidence on small and medium enterprise [SME], growth and poverty, 'does not support the contention that SMEs are particularly effective job creators.'"[27] In addition, the Bank's analysis reveals that "the size of the SME sector is not significantly associated with the income of the poorest quintile of society, the percentage of the population living below the poverty line, or the poverty gap."[28] In other words, it appears that while prosperous and thriving economies usually have a strong small and medium enterprise sector "cross-country comparisons do not indicate that SMEs exert a particularly beneficial impact on the incomes of the poor, [nor show] a significant relation between SMEs and measures of the depth and breadth of poverty."[29] In sum, if the overarching objective is poverty reduction, a simple private sector development strategy is unlikely to be sufficient. It will be necessary to target the poor geographically, in the north and northwest, where 91 per cent of households are poor and 81 per cent are extremely poor, and by sector (urban informal, agricultural, and non-farm rural).[30]

As for the resurrection of the export-assembly sector, the strategy will have to be modified if poverty reduction is the objective. Some have suggested that even if the sector were restored to 1980 levels, it would likely provide employment for only 1 per cent of the population, or about 3 per cent of the work force.[31] It would seem, therefore, that for export manufacturing to affect poverty reduction in a meaningful way, it would need to directly impact the rural sector, where the poorest Haitians live and work. In other words, the urban bias of this strategy would need to be challenged. Liisa North and John Cameron have pointed to Taiwan's development experience as a source of important lessons for agrarian societies undergoing change. Relevant to the Haitian predicament, the authors note that Taiwan's impressive and rapid agricultural and industrial growth was accompanied by a remarkable improvement in the distribution of income. Their description of the country's industrial strategy could be termed "rural-friendly":

> Decentralized rural industrialization was favored and played a critical role in expanding off-farm employment and farm family incomes. By 1971, over 50% of labor-intensive industries such as food processing, textiles, and light agricultural machinery production were located in rural areas; by 1976, that proportion had increased to 64% (Peng 1992, 113). The promotion of labor-intensive rural industry, along with public works, played a critical role in generating employment, in narrowing the income gap between urban and rural families, and in stimulating the growth of domestic demand. The massive rural to urban migration and resultant growth of shantytowns typical of most other developing countries were avoided.[32]

To be sure, Haiti is not Taiwan. The Haitian state is a fragile one that lacks the capacity to undertake the critical and highly interventionist role assumed by the Taiwanese state. Moreover, the ideological and political context for pursuing certain kinds of policies has disappeared and due to geopolitical reasons, the Haitian government will not see the massive amounts of international assistance that Taiwan received. There are however, some lessons here in terms employment generation and rural development.

Recent economic reconstruction plans advanced by international donors (the EERP of 1993–4 and the 2004 ICF) have designated export manufacturing and domestic private sector development as Haiti's engines of development. Without questioning the importance of these sectors, historical and more recent evidence raises some questions about their ability to alleviate poverty and address the sizeable gap between rich and poor. Moreover, the current approach continues to exhibit a strong urban bias—a tendency that failed to reduce poverty levels in the past. In fact, previous efforts generated greater levels of inequality between the urban and rural Haitians. As a recent 2005 UN Report on the World Social Situation points out "ignoring inequality in the pursuit of development is perilous. Focusing exclusively on economic growth and income generation as a development strategy is ineffective, as it leads to the accumulation of wealth by a few and deepens the poverty of many."[33]

The argument here is not that foreign donors should orient the bulk of their aid and loans to the agricultural sector. Given the level of environmental degradation, over-population, and increased division of land-holdings, the rural sector cannot be the country's engine of economic growth.[34] However, if poverty reduction is indeed the objective, restoring agricultural production and improving food security for rural households should be a strategic priority for international donors. Furthermore, a decentralized rural industrialization plan that situates labour-intensive industries in different parts of the country (as was the case in Taiwan) rather than around Port-au-Prince, could help achieve a much needed rural-urban balance.

Future attempts at post-conflict reconstruction and development must challenge the country's long-time pattern of economic development and, in doing so, confront the traditional structures of economic power in Haiti. Indeed, the distinguished Caribbean scholar, Sidney Mintz, has argued that if policy is geared "to sustain…the present distribution of economic power in Haiti, hardly anything can be done that could have long-range beneficial political consequences."[35] An economic development orientation that embraces and empowers those that have been traditionally left out (both politically and economically) is a necessary indispensable step. Efforts that simply repeat past practices will undoubtedly fall short.

Notes

1 This section draws heavily on the densely rich work of Michel-Rolph Trouillot, *Haiti: State against Nation: Origins & Legacy Duvalierism* (New York, Monthly Review Press, 1990).

2 Pal Sletten and Willy Egset, *Poverty in Haiti* (Oslo: Fafo, 2004), 20.

3 Daniel P. Erikson, *Haiti: Challenges in Poverty Reduction: Conference Report* (Washington, DC: Inter-American Dialogue, 2004), 4.

4 Carmen Diana Deere and Peggy Antrobus, eds., *In the Shadow of the Sun: Caribbean Development Alternatives and U.S. Policy* (Boulder, CO: Westview, 1990), 144.

5 Ibid., 175.

6 Clive Y. Thomas, *The Poor and the Powerless: Economic Policy and Change in the Caribbean* (New York: Monthly Review Press, 1988), 95.

7 Lisa McGowan, *Democracy Undermined, Economic Justice Denied: Structural Adjustment and the Aid Juggernaut in Haiti* (Washington, DC: The Development Gap, 1997), 5.

8 William I. Robinson, *Promoting Polyarchy: Globalization, US Intervention, and Hegemony* (Cambridge: Cambridge University Press, 1996), 271.

9 McGowan, *Democracy Undermined, Economic Justice Denied*, 4.

10 Michael S. Hooper, "Model Underdevelopment," NACLA Report on the Americas vol. 21, no. 3 (1987): 37; Trouillot, *Haiti: State against Nation*, 213.

11 Trouillot, *Haiti: State against Nation*, 211.

12 Ibid., 213.

13 Sidney Mintz, *Caribbean Transformations* (Baltimore: The Johns Hopkins University Press, 1989).

14 Trouillot, *Haiti: State against Nation*, 215.

15 Ibid., 216.

16 Deere and Antrobus (eds.), *In the Shadow of the Sun*, 174.

17 Trouillot, *Haiti: State against Nation*, 210.

18 Mintz, *Caribbean Transformations*, 273.

19 Gerard Caprio, «Économie et société,» *La république Haïtienne: État des lieux et perspectives*, ed. Gérard Barthélemy and Christian Girault (Paris: Editons Karthala, 1993), 286.

20 Mark Weisbrot, "Structural Adjustment in Haiti," *Monthly Review* 48 (January 1997): 28.

21 Suzy Castor, "Democracy and Society in Haiti: Structures of Domination and Resistance to Change," *Latin America Faces the Twentieth Century*, ed. Susanne Jonas and Edward McCaughan (Boulder, CO: Westview, 1994), 160.

22 Members of the mission included as well the World Bank (IBRD/IDA), United Nations Development Program (UNDP), Food and Agriculture Organization (FAO), United Nations HABITAT, United Nations Economic, Social and Cultural Organization (UNESCO), United Nations Family Planning Association (UNFPA), United Nations Fund for Children (UNICEF), United Nations Industrial Development Organization (UNIDO), World Food Program (WFP), European Union (EU), US Agency for International Development (USAID), Organization of American States (OAS), Pan American Health Organization (PAHO), World Health Organization (WHO), and Canadian International Development Agency (CIDA).

23 Weisbrot, "Structural Adjustment in Haiti," 35.

24 McGowan, *Democracy Undermined, Economic Justice Denied*, 22.

25 Ibid., 19.

26 ABT Associates, *Haiti Agribusiness Assessment Prepared for USAID* (Washington, DC: ABT Associates, 1995), cited in Ibid., 25.

27 Brian Tomlinson, "The UNDP Commission on the Private Sector and Development. Unleashing Entrepreneurship: Making Business Work for the Poor: A CCIC Commentary" (Ottawa: Canadian Council for International Cooperation, 2004), 3.

28 Thorston Beck, Asli Demirguc-Kunt, and Ross Levine, *Small and Medium Enterprises, Growth, and Poverty: Cross-Country Evidence* (Washington, DC: The World Bank, 2003), 4.

29 Ibid., 26.

30 Center for Development Information and Evaluation, *Impact Evaluation United States Agency for International Development. Providing Emergency Aid to Haiti* (Washington, DC: United States Agency for International Development, 1999), 8.

31 Matthew Creelman, "US Plan for Economic Recovery Depends Heavily on Private Sector Reactivation," *Chronicle of Latin American Economic Affairs* 10, no. 18 (1995): 3.

32 Liisa North and John Cameron, "Grassroots-based Rural Development Strategies: Ecuador in Comparative Perspective," *World Development* 28, no. 10 (2000): 1754. See also, Tso-kwein Peng, "Prices, Income, and Farm Policy in Taiwan," *Rural Development in Taiwan and Mainland China*, ed. Peter H. Calkins, Wens Chern, and Francis C. Tuan (Boulder,CO: Westview, 1992), 113.

33 "Executive Summary," *Report on the World Social Situation 2005: The Inequality Predicament* (New York: United Nations, 2005).

34 Anthony P. Maingot, "Haiti: Sovereign Consent versus State-Centric Sovereignty," *Beyond Sovereignty: Collectively Defending Democracy in the Americas*, ed. Tom Farer (Baltimore: Johns Hopkins University Press, 1996), 195–98.

35 Mintz, *Caribbean Transformations*, 86.

Justice and Security

4

Haiti's Tenuous Human
Rights Climate

ANDREW S. THOMPSON

Since the armed insurgency of February 2004 that removed President
Jean-Bertrand Aristide from office, the human rights situation in Haiti has
been in a state of crisis. At present, the country is politically polarized, and law-
lessness and violence have become common, despite the renewed presence of
international forces in the country. The human rights watchdog Amnesty
International (AI) recently found that "politically motivated arbitrary deten-
tions, ill-treatment, extrajudicial executions, deliberate and arbitrary killings
of civilians, rape, death threats and intimidation are routine and are perpe-
trated with impunity." Those carrying out these abuses include "armed gangs
with or without political ties to former President Jean-Bertrand Aristide, rogue
police officers, former rebels, demobilized members of the former Haitian
Armed Forces (FAdH)," and members of organized criminal gangs.[1]

This chapter offers a brief survey of the human rights situation in Haiti
from the emergence of Duvalierism in 1957 to the insurgency of February
2004. It is based on reports produced by international human rights organizations and the United Nations. They reveal that the protection of human
rights has not come easily to Haiti. Nor has the international community, in
its dealings with Haiti, traditionally placed a high premium on rights. Should
these trends continue once the immediate crisis has been resolved, the promotion of justice and a political and social climate favourable to international
human rights norms will be difficult and likely to encounter considerable set-
backs before the realization of any tangible improvements. Even so, a state's

commitment to the human rights of its citizens is an important indicator of its overall health and stability. Foregoing this commitment in Haiti today would likely prove counterproductive, and could one day come to be seen as a lost opportunity for a new beginning.

Human Rights Abuses under the Duvaliers, 1957–1986

The Duvalier regimes were particularly destructive for Haiti. First elected in 1957, Dr. Francois "Papa Doc" Duvalier and his infamous henchmen, the *tonton macoutes,* ruled with tremendous cruelty. Consolidating his grip on the country, he declared himself to be "President-for-life" in 1964. He ruled for another seven years, eventually relinquishing his hold on 21 April 1971 as death took him peacefully in his sleep. Systemic human rights abuses continued under his successor, his nineteen-year old son, Jean-Claude "Baby Doc" Duvalier. Despite initial efforts to disband the *macoutes,* Baby Doc's presidency was not unlike that of his father. Political opponents—journalists, human rights activists, trade unionists, and clergy—were regularly the targets of government reprisals.[2] Often they were charged with violating Haiti's Anti-Communist Law of 28 April 1969, a broad law that gave the government the authority to imprison, and even execute, anyone whom it considered to be a threat to national security.[3] These arrests, along with the subsequent trials, often violated international norms concerning both due process and the humane treatment of prisoners. Defendants were frequently denied access to a lawyer until a few days before they were scheduled to appear in court and rarely were there any witnesses to testify against them. Jurors often did not understand French, the language of the court, and some even had "connections to [government] security forces."[4] Moreover, torture and ill-treatment in Haitian prisons were common practices, as were extra-judicial executions.[5]

These abuses helped to prompt a steady exodus from the country. Prior to the late-1970s, the question of what to do about the boat people who fled the regime had not warranted much international attention; however, this began to change in 1980, as more and more boatloads began to arrive off the coasts of Florida. Responding to growing domestic pressure, the Carter Administration issued Executive Order 12244. The order permitted US authorities to establish a $100 million housing program at Fort Allen in Puerto Rico. Although the base offered temporary sanctuary, protecting Haitians from a dictatorial government was not high on the list of priorities for US officials, and little effort was made to distinguish those who qualified as Convention refugees under the terms of the 1951 *Convention relating to the Status of Refugees* and its 1967 *Protocol* from those who were fleeing Haiti's oppressive poverty.

Environmental, economic, and social instability exacerbated the already volatile political climate of the early 1980s. According to a report that was produced for the United Nations General Assembly, the 1970s had shown a significant rise in industrial production in Haiti, leading to a 23 per cent rise in Gross Domestic Product (GDP). However, any gains that came about as a result of this economic growth were short-lived. In 1981, the island of Hispaniola was hit hard by Hurricane Allen, a storm that devastated Haiti's already fragile subsistence agricultural economy. An outbreak of African Swine Fever compounded the country's economic instability. Lasting for approximately three years, the fever caused the near decimation of the pig population, eliminating one of the major sources of protein from the Haitian diet. To make matters worse, tourism fell to new lows, while the bauxite mines that produced one of the country's few mineral exports closed forever in 1982, when the last of the reserves were exhausted.[6]

The combination of political unrest and economic desperation created the conditions for an explosive and volatile situation; all that was needed was a spark. It came mid-way through the decade. In 1985, in response to growing criticism of his presidency, Jean-Claude Duvalier asked Haitians in a national referendum whether they supported the "President-for-Life" policy, including the President's "right to designate a successor."[7] Of the 2.4 million Haitians who participated in the referendum, an astonishing 99.98 per cent apparently voted in favour of the proposal (not surprisingly, few outside the government took the results seriously). By January 1986, Haitians had had enough. Fuelled by anger at the fraudulent referendum, an anti-Duvalier revolution erupted across the country. Reprisals against Duvalierists soon followed, as members of the tonton macoutes were dragged into the streets and killed by angry mobs. Sensing that all was lost, Jean-Claude Duvalier fled the country (he eventually obtained asylum in France on 7 February), thus bringing an abrupt and violent end to twenty-nine years of Duvalier rule.

The Uneasy Transition from Dictatorship to Democracy, 1986–1990

The Haitian military under General Henri Namphy stepped in to fill the vacuum left behind by Duvalier's departure. On the pretence that concrete steps needed to be taken in order to set the groundwork for a transition from dictatorship to democracy, Namphy established the National Governing Council (CNG), a body whose primary responsibilities were to schedule local and federal elections, initiate constitutional reform, and depoliticize the armed forces. Still, despite the high hopes, no new era of respect for human rights emerged from the wreckage of the 1986 revolution. That such a climate would take hold in a relatively short period of time was perhaps an unreasonable expectation; nonetheless, there was a tremendous sense of optimism, both inside and outside the country, that Haiti would soon become the western hemisphere's newest democracy. Alas, the dream never became reality. In the last half of the decade, Haiti's political climate remained plagued by instability. From 1986 to 1990, four different governments, two military and two civilian, would come to power and with each, human rights violations and violence remained the norm.[8]

Shortly into its tenure, however, the CNG presented Haitians with a new constitution and in many respects, the document represented a stark departure from the past. Among other things, it created the position of prime minister, and granted him the authority to veto any cabinet appointments. Article 266(d) of the constitution limited the military's role in law enforcement to situations in which the Haitian National Police were unable to fulfill their role in maintaining order. Article 291 barred anyone formerly associated with the Duvaliers from running for office. Once completed, the new constitution was accepted overwhelmingly in a national referendum held on 29 March 1987.

Violence among various political factions marred the months leading up to the November election. In July 1987, former macoutes, who were believed to be in league with some of Haiti's wealthy landowners, surrounded peasants from the rural town of Jean-Rabel, many of whom had affiliations with the grassroots organization *Tet Ansamn* (Heads Together), killing 140.[9] In October, lawyer and presidential candidate Yves Volel was found murdered,[10] and on 29 November, the day of the election, armed assailants gunned down thirty voters in the suburb of Carrefour Fouille in Port-au-Prince, an event that prompted a sudden halt to the election. In response, the Haitian military rounded up forty-six people, hauled them off to Fort Dimanche penitentiary and summarily executed them.[11] General Henri Namphy postponed the elections until 17 January 1988. The eventual "winner" of the election was historian François Leslie Manigat. Although the international community recognized the new government, many considered Manigat to be too close to Namphy, and remained dubious of the authenticity of the results.

By June, the human rights situation had once again descended into crisis. The situation became so severe that the UN Human Rights Commission (HRC) reported that, in the first six months of the Manigat presidency, conditions had become comparable to those of Jean-Claude Duvalier's last years in office. Indeed, it estimated that more than five hundred Haitians had been killed during this time. To make matters worse, the Commission found evidence to suggest that the tonton macoutes had reportedly re-entered the political scene "for purposes of repression."[12] Given this state of instability, it is perhaps not surprising that the Manigat regime was short-lived. Amid the violence, Namphy staged a coup, arresting officials linked to Manigat and dissolving both houses of the Haitian National Assembly; in short, rule by decree had returned to Haiti.[13]

To no one's surprise, the human rights situation continued to worsen. On 11 September 1988, armed civilians entered St. Jean Bosco Church located in La Saline, Port-au-Prince. During the mass, they attacked those inside and set fire to the building in the hope of assassinating a popular Catholic priest by the name of Jean-Bertrand Aristide.[14] While Aristide was able to escape, many were not so lucky. In total, eleven people were killed, another seventy injured. Fearing that Namphy had lost control, high-ranking officials in the army intervened; six days after the St. Jean Bosco burning, the Haitian army, under the command of Lieutenant-General Prosper Avril, deposed Namphy and his supporters.

The international community responded to the new government with cautious optimism. Soon after Avril took office, international aid to Haiti, which had been suspended under Namphy, resumed, despite reports from the HRC that the Avril government was a de facto government with neither the legal nor constitutional basis for governing, and that, like its predecessor, it was ruling by military decree.[15] Even so, governments in Canada and the United States interpreted the change in government as a sign that the political climate in Haiti was no longer dangerously unstable. Both governments began the process of repatriating the Haitian refugees who had fled the previous regime, a move that troubled officials at the Commission because the Avril government had done little to alleviate the "obstacles hindering the process of real improvement in the human rights situation in Haiti."[16] With no legitimate claim to the presidency, Avril faced considerable pressure to step down. He did so on 10 March 1990, ceding power to Judge Ertha Pascal-Trouillot, whose primary task as provisional president was to oversee a new round of elections.

On 16 December 1990 Aristide and his *Lavalas* party were elected to office in a free and fair election, winning a striking 67 per cent of the popular vote, marking an important moment for democracy in Haiti. With his victory, the transition from dictatorship to democracy appeared to have been successful. Even so, Aristide's electoral victory did not necessarily translate into an improvement to the human rights situation. Both Amnesty International and Americas Watch (later Human Rights Watch) found that the types of abuses occurring had shifted from state-endorsed violations to *déchoukage*, or mob justice. Both organizations reported that military and paramilitary personnel who had previously been protected by the state were now vulnerable to lynchings, as well as to a particularly horrific form of torture known as *Père Lebrun*, in which a burning tire was placed around the neck of the victim. Opponents of the new government were also targeted. On this issue, Aristide said very little, a silence that led both organizations to question whether his government condoned the violations.[17]

Haiti's "experiment" with democratic rule, however, was short-lived. On 30 September 1991, after only eight months in office, Aristide was forced to leave the country. Haiti had once again fallen victim to another military coup d'état.

The Return of Military Rule, 1991–1994

From 1 October 1991 to 16 October 1994, General Raoul Cédras and his *Front pour l'Avancement et le Progrès d'Haiti* (Front for the Advancement of Progress in Haiti, FRAPH) controlled Haiti with relative impunity, despite the imposition of international sanctions. As had been the case with its predecessors, human rights meant little during Cédras's rule.

The Organization of American States (OAS) was the first international governing body to condemn the coup. On 3 October 1991, it asked foreign governments and the UN Security Council to impose diplomatic sanctions and suspend all commercial relations, particularly for items that could be used by military, police and security personnel, such as arms and munitions.[18] Six days later, it sent a civilian mission to Haiti (the OAS/DEMOC), its mandate being to negotiate the terms of Aristide's potential return to office.

Meanwhile, the number of politically motivated executions began to rise. During the initial days of the coup, Amnesty International reported that Cédras and his forces had killed six Haitians in the city of Gonaïves, another thirty to forty people in the district of Lamentin 54, and more than fifty Haitians from the slums of Cité Soleil in Port-au-Prince. In addition to these murders, FRAPH members had descended on and fired shots into Aristide's *Lafamni Selavi* orphanage, and summarily arrested approximately thirty Lavalas supporters from the districts of Carrefour Feuille and Les Cayes.[19]

By early 1992, the crisis worsened. Three months into the coup, Amnesty International found that Cédras began eliminating through force all grassroots organizations, both political and non-political. He also re-established the authority of the macoutes and the chefs de section, the old regional police chiefs of the Duvalier era whom Aristide had disarmed, in the rural areas of the country; issued "hit lists" on the radio; burned the homes of Aristide supporters; attacked both domestic and foreign clergy; permitted his soldiers to perform rape as a "weapon of terror"; and targeted journalists who were critical of the regime.[20]

One of the consequences of the coup was a massive increase in the number of boat people fleeing Haiti. In February 1992, the United Nations HRC reported that more than twenty thousand refugees had fled the "violence, torture and military coercion" of the FRAPH.[21] In May, estimates were that the number of Haitians who had left the country had reached thirty-four thousand. To stem the exodus, President George Bush (Sr.) issued Executive Order 12807, *The Interdiction of Illegal Aliens*. The order instructed US Coast Guard officials to repatriate all Haitian boat people without first screening them to see if any qualified as Convention refugees. Human rights groups and the UN were intensely critical of US policy, accusing Washington of engaging in refoulement, the return of refugees to a place where their lives or freedoms might be endangered.[22]

To resolve the boat people crisis, and set the process in motion for his return to office, Aristide met with the Haitian Parliamentary Negotiating Commission, the body charged with finding a suitable compromise to the conflict. On 11 March 1992, Haiti's Permanent Representative to the United Nations, Fritz Longchamp, submitted an agreement to the UN General Assembly that was signed by Aristide and two representatives of the Negotiating Commission.[23] The agreement was significant for a number of reasons. Among other things, it called for the "establishment and consolidation of democratic institutions," "respect for the principle of the separation of powers in accordance with the Constitution," the separation of the police and armed forces, and the creation of an environment that guaranteed civil liberties and facilitated "the free functioning of political parties and civic organizations in respect for the Constitution." It also required Aristide to choose a new "consensus" prime minister in consultation with the respective presidents of the Senate and the Chamber of Deputies. Second, the parties involved agreed to "proclaim a general amnesty, save for common criminals," and denounce "any intervention by foreign armed forces in the settlement of Haitian affairs."[24] Regrettably these last two conditions, while expeditious, reinforced a climate of impunity, and suggested that the perpetrators of the coup were beyond the reach of the justice system.

Ultimately, this compromise did not matter. Following the Commission's return to Haiti, Cédras reneged on the deal. The OAS's failure to broker an agreement between the two sides reflected wider criticisms that the trade embargo had, by most measures, been a failure. The sanctions had not been well enforced, as neither the Dominican Republic nor a number of European countries had agreed to cut off trade to Haiti. Cédras and his security forces had responded to the sanctions by extracting "protection" money from the population, the poorest of whom were hit particularly hard. In a clear show of defiance, he staged new parliamentary elections on 18 January 1993. All this time, "extra-judicial executions, arbitrary and illegal arrests, torture and ill-treatment" remained frequent.[25]

A resolution to the crisis did not begin to emerge until late June 1993. At the urging of the "Friends of Haiti" (the United States, France, Canada, and Venezuela), both sides agreed to another round of negotiations, this time to be held at Governors Island, New York. Following six days of intense talks, both sides signed the appropriately named Governors Island Agreement, a deal which laid the groundwork for a political truce to the conflict. In exchange for reaffirming Cédras's amnesty and lifting the economic sanctions, Aristide would be allowed to select a new prime minister and return to office on 30 October 1993. The agreement also opened the door for considerable international involvement in shaping Haiti's post-conflict environment. It called for a resumption of international development aid, and substantial assistance in reforming the country's police and judicial systems. Moreover, the agreement authorized the UN Mission to Haiti (UNMIH) and the joint OAS/UN Civilian Mission in Haiti (MICIVIH) to verify that both parties were living up their respective commitments.[26]

While the Governors Island Agreement was a diplomatic victory, it was noticeably ambiguous about the issue of protecting human rights.[27] To compensate for these deficiencies, the United Nations submitted a list of additional demands to Cédras and the Haitian Parliament on 16 July, known as the New York Pact. The list included an end to arbitrary arrests and torture, the release of all political prisoners, respect for fundamental freedoms, compensation to the victims of the coup, and a reassurance that all those who were elected in the 18 January election "refrain from occupying their parliamentary seats until such time as the constitutional institution empowered to consider [the legitimacy of the election] has rendered its verdict."[28] All of these new stipulations were to be implemented prior to Aristide's return. To give the Pact some teeth, the Security Council voted in favour of a total oil and arms embargo.

Again, these efforts were all for nought. By autumn 1993, it was clear that Cédras was unwilling to comply with the demands of the international community.[29] Those who made up the de facto government refused to cooperate with UNMIH peacekeepers. Perhaps the most flagrant incident came on 11 October, as armed protestors prevented the roughly two hundred Canadian and American troops on board the USS *Harlan County* from docking.[30] The UN Security Council reacted to the event by passing Resolution 873 on 13 October, which once again called upon the international community to halt all shipments of petroleum products and arms to Haiti (the sanctions of 16 July had been lifted temporarily on 27 August).[31] Again, Cédras remained defiant. The following day, François-Guy Malary, Aristide's minister of justice, was assassinated. Conceding that a diplomatic solution was unlikely, the Security Council passed a second resolution, Resolution 875, which authorized the body to "consider further necessary measures to ensure full compliance with the provisions of relevant Security Council resolutions."[32]

Meanwhile, growing criticism of the United States government's treatment of the Haitian boat people was making it increasingly difficult for Washington to allow the crisis to continue. In the early months of 1994, the Congressional Black Caucus (CBC) called on the Clinton administration to bring US policy toward Haitian boat people in line with the norms and standards found in international law.[33] On 12 April, Randall Robinson, the executive director of the organization TransAfrica, began what would eventually become a twenty-seven-day hunger strike in protest of the US government's refusal to revoke Executive Order 12807. Supporting Robinson was the newly formed Artists for Democracy in Haiti, a group that included such Hollywood elites as "Jonathan Demme, Robert De Niro, Paul Newman, Susan Sarandon, Harry Belafonte, Gregory Peck, Julia Roberts, Richard Gere, Robin Williams, Joanne Woodward, Jason Robards, and Spike Lee."[34]

The criticisms were not unwarranted. There existed considerable evidence to suggest that US policy had resulted in a number of cases of refoulement. For approximately two years, Amnesty International had been tracking the cases of seventeen Haitians who had been arrested following their repatriation. One was a man by the name of Oman Désanges, president of the Association des Jeunes Progressistes de Martissant (Young Progressive Association of Martissant); Désanges was later murdered after Immigration Naturalization Service (INS) officials, who had initially agreed to grant him asylum, mistakenly returned him to Haiti.[35] Despite the criticisms, the Clinton Administration was slow to alter its policy. Only in May did it agree to provide safe-haven to the refugees, announcing in mid-June that it had negotiated an agreement with the Jamaican government that permitted the INS to screen claimants aboard the USS *Comfort*, which was to be stationed just off the coast of Jamaica.

Events continued to go badly for the OAS and the United Nations. In late April, the UN Secretary General's office reported to the General Assembly that, despite the presence of MICIVIH observers, the "humanitarian situation [was] deteriorating," while the "human rights situation has grown significantly worse over the past three months."[36] This assessment was prompted in part by the massacre that took place between 18 and 22 April in Raboteau, a poor village near the coastal city of Gonaïves. Raboteau was a pro-Aristide town with strong ties to the Lavalas Party. Military and paramilitary forces had descended on the small town, and attacked its residents. At the end of the four days, twenty people were estimated to have been killed, and scores of others injured.[37] In response, the OAS and UN issued a joint ultimatum to Cédras on 6 May: if he did not comply with the Governors Island Agreement by 21 May, they would call for a total economic embargo that would encompass all goods save humanitarian aid. Cédras balked at the threat. In response, the UN and OAS finally convinced the Dominican Republic to assist in halting the shipment of illegal goods across the Haitian-Dominican border.

Cédras responded by expelling MICIVIH on 11 July following the expiration of its first mandate, removing any international monitoring presence in Haiti. Left with few other options, the UN Security Council issued Resolution 940 on 31 July, which called for the creation of a Multinational Force (MNF) under Chapter VII of the United Nations Charter, its mission to enforce the terms of the Governors Island Agreement.[38]

Amnesty International had a number of reservations about the MNF's presence in Haiti. While the organization remained neutral on the question of whether military force was necessary, it feared that intervention would do little to curb the human rights violations being committed. One concern was that the MNF, if not careful, could potentially foster a wave of déchoukage that would sweep across the country. As had been the case in 1986 against the macoutes, the possibility remained that civilians might attempt to seek reprisals against military and paramilitary personnel for the crimes of the last three years. Equally troubling was the prospect that governments in the region might assume that it was safe for Haitians that had fled the coup to return home, an assumption that, given the circumstances, seemed overly optimistic.[39]

The deadlock between Cédras and the international community was finally broken in September 1994. That month, President Bill Clinton, with the MNF ready to invade if deemed necessary, sent a high-level delegation to Haiti consisting of former President Jimmy Carter, former Chairman of the Joint Chiefs of Staff Colin Powell, and Senator Sam Nunn, the chairman of the US Senate Armed Services Committee. There they presented the de facto regime with an ultimatum to cede power or face invasion. With little other option, Cédras's representative conceded defeat, although not before an agreement was reached that would allow US and Haitian soldiers to maintain order collectively, and permit Cédras to flee to Panama.

International Engagement and Human Rights after the Coup, 1994–2004

Aristide returned to Haiti on 15 October 1994, bringing a formal end to the crisis but for Haitians, as well as the international community, the task of solidifying democratic rule had only just begun. From the mid-1990s to the early 2000s, the international community remained actively engaged in Haiti. Unfortunately, the involvement produced few meaningful or lasting results.[40]

The mid- to late-1990s saw a gradual, and arguably premature, reduction in the UN/OAS presence in Haiti. As mandated by Resolution 940, UNMIH took over from the MNF in January 1995, its force comprising roughly six thousand troops and almost eight hundred police officers. Over the next five years, UNMIH would consist of three follow-up missions: the UN Support Mission in Haiti (UNSMIH) (June 1996 to July 1997); the UN Transition Mission in Haiti (UNTMIH) (July 1997 to November 1997), a mission consisting almost exclusively of police officers; and the UN Civilian Police Mission in Haiti (MIPONUH) (November 1997 to March 2000). After MIPONUH's and MICIVIH's mandates expired, the UN implemented the short-lived International Support Mission in Haiti (MICAH), a program that ended in February 2001, largely due to funding constraints.[41]

During this time, the human rights situation in Haiti improved only marginally, although there were some significant achievements. Upon his return, one of Aristide's initiatives had been to disband the army on 31 December 1995. Also, the national election that saw the peaceful transfer of power from Aristide to René Préval on 7 February 1996 was considered by most observers to be generally free and fair. In addition to this, some prison reform did take place. Also in February 1996, the National Truth and Justice Commission that Aristide had established two years earlier to investigate the human rights abuses committed during the coup, submitted its final report to the government.[42] Even so, a number of systemic problems remained unresolved. Déchoukage and a lack of judicial independence continued to beset the justice system. Moreover, little effort was expended to bring perpetrators of past abuses to justice, while political violence and police abuses were common.[43] Amnesty International contended, and with good reason, that this general willingness to tolerate a culture of impunity would lead to problems in the future.[44]

The Human Rights Situation prior to February 2004

Despite some improvements, systemic abuses persisted during Aristide's second term as president. The judicial system continued to be plagued by serious problems, despite assistance from MICIVIH. These included widespread corruption, inadequate resources and training for officials, and, perhaps most troubling of all, considerable interference from the executive branch of the government.[45] Concerns about transparency and impartiality were not restricted to the judiciary; politicization, abuse, and an overall lack of professionalism were common within the Haitian National Police (HNP) as well.

By 2004, anti-Aristide sentiment had risen considerably, with many sectors of the Haitian population calling on him to step down. To curb the dissent, Aristide's government used the police and employed armed gangs known as chimères to silence its opponents, a practice that had been going on for much of Aristide's second term as President.[46] This strategy only fuelled opposition to his government. Under the command of Guy Philippe, a former army officer and HNP commissioner, and Louis-Jodel Chamblain, the ex-second-in-command of the FRAPH, a group of insurgents consisting of former members of the disbanded Haitian military (FAdH), former FRAPH, as well as a group of paramilitary fighters known as the "Cannibal Army," launched an attack in Gonaïves on 5 February. They targeted police stations, prisons, and court houses, looting and destroying many. Government officials and members of the HNP who feared for their safety fled the area. Violence quickly spread to other parts of the country as the insurgency gained momentum. Even the former Chefs de Section, the rural police chiefs dating back to the Duvalier era, joined the ranks of the anti-Aristide rebellion. So too did many of the prisoners whom the insurgents had freed. Before long, they had gained control over much of the Northern and central regions of country. Predictably, Philippe and his supporters set their sights on the capital.

In the midst of the growing chaos and violence, a number of significant and controversial events occurred on 29 February. First, Aristide left Haiti— under circumstances that are still being contested to this day—on a US plane destined for the Central African Republic. Second, the UN Security Council passed Resolution 1529, which called for the creation of a Multinational Interim Force (MIF), again under Chapter VII of the UN Charter. Consisting of troops from the US, Canada, France, and Chile, its mandate was to restore order for a period of three months.[47] Third, steps were taken for the creation of a transitional government. With Aristide out of the country, Supreme Court President Boniface Alexandre was sworn in as interim president. Nine days later, upon the recommendation of the Haitian Council of the Wise, Gérard

Latortue, a former economist with the United Nations, was named prime minister of the new transitional government.[48]

The Human Rights Situation since February 2004

Despite the presence of the UN Stabilization Mission in Haiti (MINUSTAH) forces, the human rights situation in Haiti has remained perilous and in need of strengthening.[49] A deeply ingrained culture of impunity;[50] widespread police abuses including arbitrary arrests, torture, and extrajudicial executions;[51] a judiciary that lacks independence; high levels of criminal activity; and an overall climate of insecurity are but a few of the immediate and long-term challenges that are in need of remedy.[52]

The prevalence and widespread access to small arms has also had tremendous implications for the human rights climate in Haiti. Indeed, a number of non-governmental organizations have argued that the most pressing issue facing Haiti at the moment is the proliferation of approximately 170,000 small arms, many of which are in the hands of non-state actors.[53] Both the UN Security Council and the Latortue government recognized the urgency of this problem, although the lack of results to date has been disappointing.[54] In February 2005, the process began of demobilizing members of the former military through a National Commission on Disarmament. Unfortunately, the Commission's initial results have not been encouraging; the few guns that have been collected are often old, their utility very much in doubt.[55]

The question—and it is a big one—is how to disarm the various actors that have access to small arms. The answer, of course, is neither straightforward nor obvious. The right to own a firearm is protected in the Haitian constitution, as long as it is registered with the authorities. Moreover, as Keith Krause of Small Arms Survey (SAS) Project has argued, "small arms are *social artefacts*" that are "embedded in complex social systems" requiring "a nuanced understanding of the social and economic context of weapons possession and use."[56] The challenge will be to develop a Disarmament, Demobilization and Reintegration Program (DDR) that addresses the unique circumstances in Haiti that have led to the high demand for weapons in the first place. Otherwise, Haiti's long term prospects for stability and respect for human rights will likely continue to be tenuous at best.

In March 2004, UN Secretary General Kofi Annan wrote in the *Wall Street Journal* that "the most important lesson [coming out of Haiti] is that there can be no quick exit. Haiti will need our resources and our support for a long time. The current crisis is at least as much the result of irresponsible behaviour by the Haitian political class as of omissions or failures in previous international efforts." He continued, "The stakes are high—above all for Haitians, but also for us. Getting it right this time means doing things differently. Above all, it means keeping international attention and resources engaged for the long haul."[57] Whether Haitian authorities and the international community heed the Secretary General's warning remains to be seen. Any efforts to improve the overall state of human rights in Haiti will not be easy and there will likely be a temptation to favour expeditious solutions over genuine reform. But strengthening state institutions for the purposes of promoting rights is a necessary and worthwhile investment, the dividend being that Haiti may one day abandon its current unstable and violent path.

Notes

1 Amnesty International, "Disarmament Delay, Justice Denied," AMR 36/005/2005, 28 July 2005, 1.

2 In October 1980, Haitian authorities arrested twenty-six people, charging each with violating the country's Anti-Communist Law. One of the individuals arrested was Sylvio Claude, president of the Parti Démocrate Chrétien Haitien (PDCH). According to PDCH, Claude was arrested for distributing a picture of Jean-Claude Duvalier alongside other foreign leaders who had recently been removed from office, a picture that the government interpreted as a threat to the president. He was rearrested on 9 October 1983, this time for running in an election against a known tonton macoute. Among the others who were arrested were radio journalist Yvens Paul and Lafontant Joseph, Secretary General of *la Ligue Haitienne des Droits Humains*. Amnesty International, "Haiti: Human Rights Violations, October 1980 to October 1981," (London: Amnesty International Publications, November 1981), 1–8. See also, Americas Watch/Lawyers Committee for International Human Rights, "Election 1984: Duvalier Style: A Report on Human Rights in Haiti Based on a Mission of Inquiry" (New York: Americas Watch, 1984), 4, 11.

3 Haiti's Anti-Communist Law covered "all crimes against the security of the state, punishable by the death penalty."

4 Amnesty International, "Haiti: Human Rights Violations, October 1980 to October 1981," 5–7.

5 Shortly into Jean-Claude Duvalier's tenure, Amnesty International reported that Haitian prisoners were subjected to "clubbing to death, maiming of the ears and genitals, food deprivation to the point of starvation, and the insertion of red-hot pokers into the back passage." In addition to these abuses, prison conditions were highly unsanitary; diseases such as tuberculosis, malaria and chronic diarrhoea were often left untreated. See Amnesty International, "Report on the Situation of Political Prisoners in Haiti, 1973" (London: Amnesty International Publications, 1973), 1–3.

6 According to a United Nations General Assembly Report in 1986, only one half of Haitian land was considered to be arable. It also noted that "rainfall is irregular and the country is subject to periodic severe droughts and occasional hurricanes. Deforestation and soil erosion have become critical problems, reducing even further the

land available for cultivation." Infant mortality was also 120/1000 births, malnutrition was systemic, and the economy was plagued by "an acute shortage of skilled manpower" United Nations General Assembly, *Special Economic and Disaster Relief Assistance: Assistance to Haiti: Report of the Secretary General* General Assembly A/40/432, 25 October 1985, 1–9.

7 The referendum also asked whether Haitians approved of "the creation of the post of Prime Minister; an increase in legislative influence over the government; and an official encouraging of the development of political pluralism." Americas Watch/The National Coalition for Haitian Refugees, "Haiti: Human Rights under Hereditary Dictatorship" (New York: Americas Watch, October 1985), 2.

8 General Henri Namphy (7 February 1986 to 17 January 1988, 20 June to 18 September 1988) took control of the country immediately after the revolution. Leslie Manigat (18 January to 20 June 1988) won what many considered to be a fixed election and was displaced by Namphy after six months in office. Lt-General Prosper Avril (18 September 1988 to 11 March 1990) staged a coup d'état against Namphy. Finally Judge Ertha Pascal Trouillot (10 March to 16 December 1990) was appointed by Avril. Many observers considered her to be a puppet leader for the military.

9 Amnesty International, "Haiti: Current Concerns," AMR 36/41/88 (London: Amnesty International Publications, November 1988), 21.

10 United Nations, ECOSOC, E/CN.4/1988/NGO/48, 16 February 1988, 2.

11 Amnesty International, "Haiti: Current Concerns," 22. See also Amnesty International, "Haiti: Deaths in Detention, Torture and Inhumane Prison Conditions," AMR 36/35/87 (London: Amnesty International Publications, December 1987), 1–8.

12 United Nations, ECOSOC, E/CN.4/1988/NGO/6, 10 June 1988.

13 Amnesty International, "Haiti: Current Concerns," 3.

14 Amnesty International, "Haiti: Current Concerns," 3.

15 See United Nations, ECOSOC, E/CN.4/1989/40, 6 February 1989.

16 On 23 October 1989, Minister of Employment and Immigration Barbara McDougall announced to the House of Commons that the government was prepared to deport fifty Haitian refugee claimants on the grounds that it was safe for them to return to Haiti. See Canada, House of Commons, *Hansard,* 25 October 1989, 5052.

The Human Rights Commission concluded that some of the problems plaguing Haiti were: "(i) an ineffective judicial system; (ii) the militarization of the rural areas; (iii) the failure to separate the army and the police forces; and (iv) the fact that those responsible for the principal massacres, in particular those on 29 November 1987 and 11 September 1988, have not been put on trial." See United Nations, ECOSOC Council, E/CN.4/1990/44, 23 January 1990.

17 One of the victims of Père Lebrun was Josue Lafance, a parliamentarian who was about to bring a vote of no confidence against Lavalas prime minister René Préval. Amnesty International, "Haiti: Human Rights Violations in the Aftermath of the Coup d'État," AMR 36/09/91 (London: Amnesty International Publications, 1991), 3. See also Americas Watch, "A Report by Americas Watch, and the National Coalition for Haitian Refugees and Caribbean Rights," (New York: Americas Watch/National Coalition for Haitian Refugees, 1 November 1991), 6.

18 See United Nations Security Council, S/23109, 3 October 1991, 3–4.

19 Amnesty International, "Haiti: Human Rights Violations in the Aftermath of the Coup d'État," 2.

20 A common form of torture was a "djak," a practice in which a "baton is wedged under the thighs and over the arms of the victim who is then beaten repeatedly." Amnesty International, "Haiti: The Human Rights Tragedy: Human Rights Violations since the Coup," AMR 36/03/92 (London: Amnesty International Publications, January 1992), 2–39, particularly p. 24.

21 United Nations, ECOSOC Council, E/CN.4/1992/SR.45, 3 March 1992, 5.

22 By August, estimates suggested that the number of boat people intercepted by the US Coast Guard since October 1991 had risen to 38,000. See Amnesty International, "Haiti: Human Rights Held to Ransom," AMR 36/41/92, August 1992, 26.

Forced repatriation by US authorities was not a new practice. In September 1981, the United States signed a bilateral agreement with the Jean-Claude Duvalier government, which "permitted US authorities to intercept outside US territorial waters Haitians trying to reach the USA and return them to Haiti." See Amnesty International, "Haiti: The Human Rights Tragedy: Human Rights Violations since the Coup," 38. See also, E/CN.4/1992/SR.45, p. 5; United Nations General Assembly, A/RES/46/138, 9 March 1992; and Americas Watch, "Half the Story—The Skewed US Monitoring of Repatriated Haitian Refugees," (New York: Americas Watch in conjunction with the National Coalition for Haitian Refugees, 30 June 1992), 3, 9–13.

23 In addition to Aristide, the two representatives were Déjean Belizaire, President of the Senate and the Haitian Parliamentary Negotiating Commission, and Alexandre Médard, President of the Chamber of Deputies and Vice-President of the Parliamentary Negotiating Commission.

24 United Nations General Assembly, A/46/891, 11 March 1992, 1–3.

25 Amnesty International, "Haiti: Human Rights Held to Ransom," 3. See also United Nations Security Council Resolution 841 (1993), 16 June 1993.

26 For a text of the Governors Island Agreement, see Report of the United Nations Secretary General, S/26063, 12 July 1993, 2–3.

Established on 9 February 1993, MICIVIH's primary responsibility was to monitor the human rights situation in Haiti. See also United Nations Security Council, Resolution 841 (1993), 16 June 1993.

27 The final paragraph of the Governors Island Agreement stated: "The President of the Republic and the Commander-in-Chief agree that these agreements constitute a satisfactory solution to the Haitian crisis and the beginning of a process of national reconciliation. They pledge to cooperate fully in the peaceful transition to a stable and lasting democratic society in which all Haitians will be able to live in a climate of freedom, justice, security and respect for human rights."

28 Report of the United Nations Secretary General, S/26297, 13 August 1993, 1–3.

29 See United Nations Security Council, Resolution 861 (1993), 27 August 1993.

30 Ronald I. Perusse, *Haitian Democracy Restored, 1991–1995* (New York: University Press of America Inc. 1995), 55.

31 United Nations Security Council, Resolution 873 (1993), 13 October 1993.

32 United Nations Security Council, Resolution 875 (1993), 16 October 1993.

33 The CBC actually submitted two bills to the US Government, H.R. No. 4114 and H.R. No. 3663. The former, entitled the "Governors Island Reinforcement Act of 1994," called on the Clinton administration to bring an end to the repatriation agreement between the United States and Haiti that had been signed in 1981. The second, the "Haitian Refugee Fairness Act" called for the State Department to incor-

porate international law into the ways in which it processed those Haitians who had fled the country during the coup. See Amnesty International, "USA/Haiti: The Price of Rejection—Human Rights Consequences for Rejected Haitian Asylum-Seekers," (London: Amnesty International Publications, May 1994), 2.

34 Amnesty International, "USA/Haiti: The Price of Rejection—Human Rights Consequences for Rejected Haitian Asylum-Seekers," 3.

35 Ibid., p. 6.

36 Report of the Secretary General of the United Nations, A/48/931, 29 April 1994, 7.

37 Amnesty International, "Haiti: Obliterating justice, overturning of sentences for Raboteau massacre by Supreme Court is a huge step backwards," Public Statement, AMR 36/006/2005, 26 May 2005.

38 The MNF's mandate was "to use all necessary means to facilitate the departure from Haiti of the military leadership, consistent with the Governors Island Agreement, the prompt return of the legitimately elected President and the restoration of the legitimate authorities of the Government of Haiti, and to establish and maintain a secure and stable environment that will permit implementation of the Governors Island Agreement, on the understanding that the cost of implementing this temporary operation will be borne by the participating Member States." United Nations Security Council, S/RES/940, 31 July 1994, 2.

According to Sebastian von Einsiedel and David M. Malone, Resolution 940 was the "first and only instance of the Security Council authorizing the use of force to effect the restoration of democracy within a member state." See Sebastian von Einsiedel and David M. Malone, "Haiti," in *The UN Security Council: From the Cold War to the 21st Century*, ed. David M. Malone (London: Lynne Rienner, 2004), 467.

39 Amnesty International also objected to the fact that Resolution 940 said nothing about the need to "protect human rights in the context of any eventual invasion." Amnesty International, "Haiti: On the Horns of a Dilemma: Military Repression or Foreign Invasion?" AMR 36/33/94 (London: Amnesty International Publications, August 1994), i, 18–24.

40 Malone and von Einsiedel have argued that "the case of Haiti presents an instance in which UN operations were broadly successful—yet the patient failed to recover." "Haiti," 467.

41 Ibid., 477.

42 See République d'Haïti, «Rapport de la Commission Nationale de Vérité et de Justice», February 1996. Available at: http://www.haiti.org/truth/table.htm. Accessed 15 January, 2006.

43 Amnesty International, "Haiti: A Question of Justice," AMR 36/01/96, (London: Amnesty International Publications, January 1996), 8–10.

44 Mid-way through Préval's term, the organization warned that "the Haitian Government has so far failed to establish a strong legal framework, based on international human rights standards, that is capable of guaranteeing the right to unimpeded access to justice for the victims of human rights abuses, both past and present. Amnesty International believes that, if not tackled with urgency, their failure to do so may have dire consequences for the respect and protection of human rights in Haiti for many years to come and will continue to undermine progress made in other fields." Amnesty International, "Haiti: Still Crying Out for Justice," AMR 36/02/98, (London: Amnesty International Publications, 1998), 2.

45 Amnesty International, "Haiti: Breaking the cycle of violence: A last chance for Haiti," AMR 36/038/2004 (London: Amnesty International Publications, June 2004), 5.

46 Amnesty International, "Haiti: Disarmament Delayed, Justice Denied," AMR 36/005/2005 (London: Amnesty International Publications, 28 July 2005), 2.

47 United Nations Security Council, Resolution 1529, S/RES/1529 (2004), 29 February 2004.

48 The Council of the Wise is a group of seven advisors consisting of members from a range of sectors of Haitian society.

49 MINUSTAH replaced the MIF on 1 June 2004. Established under United Nations Security Council Resolution 1542 on 30 April 2004, MINUSTAH called for an international force consisting of 1,622 civilian police and 6,700 peacekeepers. Like the MIF, it too was a Chapter VII mission, its mandate to secure a stable environment, support the transitional government, vet the Haitian National Police, promote human rights, and engage in a nation-wide Disarmament, Demobilization and Reintegration Program (DDR). See United Nations Security Council, Resolution 1542, S/RES/1542 (2004), 30 April 2004. Due to continued instability and the deteriorating human rights situation, the United Nations Security Council adopted Resolution 1576 on 29 November 2004, which extended MINUSTAH's mission to 1 June 2005. See United Nations Security Council, Resolution 1576, S/RES/1576 (2004), 29 November 2004.

    By May 2005, MINUSTAH consisted of about 7,400 troops, while CivPol was made up of 1622 police officers.

50 Amnesty International, "Haiti: Obliterating justice, overturning of sentences for Raboteau massacre by Supreme Court is a huge step backwards," Public Statement, AMR 36/006/2005, 26 May 2005.

51 See Paragraph 8, United Nations Security Council, Resolution 1608, S/RES/1608 (2005), 22 June 2005. Paragraph 10 "*Urges* the Transitional Government to conduct thorough and transparent investigations into cases of human rights violations, particularly those allegedly involving HNP officers; *requests* that in order to support this effort MINUSTAH make the Joint Special Investigation Unit operational as soon as possible."

52 See Amnesty International, "Haiti: Breaking the cycle of violence: A last chance for Haiti"; Amnesty International, "Haiti: Disarmament delayed, justice denied."

53 The International Crisis Group has called on the international community to "carry out a forced disarmament campaign against any groups that do not participate in the negotiated disarmament process, including former military personnel, and, simultaneously, work closely with the National Disarmament Commission to ensure implementation of a comprehensive DDR strategy." See International Crisis Group, "Spoiling Security in Haiti" Latin America/Caribbean Report N°13 31 May 2005; and International Crisis Group, "Can Haiti Hold Elections in 2005?" Latin America/Caribbean Briefing N°8, 3 August 2005.

    Keith Krause, the Director of the Small Arms Survey (SAS) Project of the Strategic and International Security Studies Programme of the Graduate Institute of International Studies in Geneva, Switzerland, has written that the central challenge today facing Haiti is arguably "insecurity stemming primarily (but not exclusively) from the proliferation and misuse of small arms and light weapons." Keith Krause, "Small Arms, Big Killers," in *Irrelevant or Indispensable? The United Nations in the*

21st Century, ed. Paul Heinbecker and Patricia Goff (Waterloo, ON: Wilfrid Laurier University Press, 2005), 105.

54 See United Nations Security Council, Resolution 1608, S/RES/1608 (2005), 22 June 2005.

55 Amnesty International, "Haiti: Disarmament delayed, justice denied," 6–7.

56 Krause, "Small Arms, Big Killers," 106.

57 Kofi Annan, "In Haiti for the Long Haul," *Wall Street Journal,* 16 March 2004. See also, Amnesty International, "Haiti: Breaking the Cycle of Violence," 15.

5

Reflections on the Situation in Haiti and the Ongoing UN Mission

COL. JACQUES MORNEAU

This chapter examines, through a military lens, the situation in Haiti between January and July 2005. The perspective advanced is a personal one, informed by my position as the former Chief of Staff (cos) of the UN Stabilization Mission in Haiti (MINUSTAH) Military Force during those months. The chapter begins with a brief description of the country during this period, stressing the key challenges, followed by a discussion of MINUSTAH's functions, including Canada's contribution to the Mission, and concludes with a set of reflections and recommendations.

Haiti's Present Outlook

The situation in Haiti is marked by political, social, economic, ecological, and security problems. In order for MINUSTAH to succeed it will have to address these interrelated problems simultaneously. The challenges are formidable and the barriers to success are many. One obstacle lies with the Haitian public sector which is unable to deliver services to the population because of historic and endemic corruption and insufficient resources at the national, regional, and municipal levels. Consequently, basic services such as road maintenance, electricity, running water, water purification, health and education are not available to many Haitians.

The opinions expressed in this chapter are those of the author only and do not represent the official policy of Canada's Department of National Defence.

The justice and penitentiary systems are also completely dysfunctional and in urgent need of reform, which should be carried out in concert with reform of the country's police force, the Haitian National Police (HNP). Most of the detainees in Haitian jails have neither been formally accused nor received due process; a large number have been in jail for long periods of time and have yet to be tried. Moreover, many criminals arrested by MINUSTAH and turned over to the police/justice systems are released without any proper prosecution because some judges are afraid to press charges, and others are sympathetic to the detainees or are simply bought.

The HNP is the only law enforcement agency in Haiti; there is no army, nor are there independent municipal or provincial police forces. Reforming the HNP is a major challenge, one that will take many years. In the meantime, the only existing law enforcement entity in the country has very serious deficiencies and is unable to maintain law and order on its own.

One of these deficiencies is a huge shortage of officers. Of the six thousand officers who receive paycheques, only approximately four thousand are available for police duties. The appropriate number of officers for a country with the population the size of Haiti's would be twelve thousand. Presently the HNP, assisted by UN Police, is graduating one thousand new officers per year; however, it will take another six to eight years to reach the desired number. Even if the HNP eventually reaches its objective of twelve thousand police officers, with a population of approximately 8.5 million inhabitants, Haiti will still in all likelihood be under-policed (New York City, which has a population of eight million, has forty-four thousand police officers). The HNP also lacks vehicles, armaments, communication systems, and many of its installations were destroyed during the anti-Aristide insurgency of 2004 or during previous crises. Due to their small numbers, there are many cities and municipalities without any HNP presence.

With an unemployment rate of more than 80 per cent, Haiti is highly susceptible to crime, which is often driven by desperation or simply the need to survive. New York's current unemployment rate is less than 5 per cent, but, despite of its low unemployment rate, a very large professional, well-paid, and well-equipped police force, New York still has a fairly high crime rate. The point is that no UN Mission, regardless of the size or capability of its forces, would be able to completely eliminate crime in the country. The question is: "What is an acceptable level of crime considering the appalling living conditions that Haitian's are forced to endure?" The existing HNP is also plagued by corruption, with a number of its members associated with illegal groups. Many were either accomplices or have committed illegal activities themselves such as kidnapping, extortion, and drug trafficking, or have been associated with the gangs like the *chimères,* and with criminal elements of the ex-military. Also problematic is the fact that some HNP have employed excessive violence during crowd control operations or have been responsible for human rights abuses. Granted, the HNP has had to operate in a country that suffers from chronic political instability; nonetheless, at times, the force has been politicized.

Due to these realities, it has been difficult for MINUSTAH to work with HNP officers, many of whom are unco-operative and unreliable. On many occasions MINUSTAH was forced to abort planned joint operations with the police because some of its elements had leaked operational information. Perhaps more troubling is that the HNP has lost the confidence of the general population; it is not an exaggeration to say that it is hated by some sectors of society. The UN Police mandate is *to assist* the HNP; it therefore has no executive authority to arrest and prosecute criminals. This is one of the major weaknesses of the MINUSTAH Mission.

Haiti also faces a chaotic socio-economic situation. Underdevelopment has meant that a staggering 80 per cent of the population live below the poverty line, and, as noted earlier, public services are almost non-existent. Schools run by NGOs or religious groups are superior to public education, which is poor in quality and limited in scope. Similarly, health and sanitation conditions are appalling due to the heaps of garbage left uncollected in the streets and canals, and a serious lack of medical services. The country also faces major ecological problems, such as massive deforestation. Due to extreme poverty, the population has been forced to cut down the few trees left to make charcoal, which they use for cooking. This deforestation has contributed directly to the erosion of the arable soil, resulting in a constant diminution of agricultural output, compounding the shortage of food, and amplifying the effects of floods during the rainy season. Every year many lives are lost to floods, and the existing limited infrastructure is damaged or destroyed beyond repair. These environmental problems are intensified by a lack of water purification systems and the absence of a functioning garbage collection system.

The main security problems during 2005 were initially caused by ex-military members, who are commonly referred to the ExFadH. Following a number of MINUSTAH offensive operations in March and April 2005 against ExFadH members, who had illegally occupied police stations in Terre Rouge and Petit Goäve, efforts were made to incorporate them into the Disarmament, Demobilization and Reintegration (DDR) process. The Transitional Government of Haiti (TGOH) promised to pay these ex-soldiers their lost salaries and pensions and provide them with jobs. Unfortunately, it was unable to keep its promises. Consequently, the ExFadH have become dissatisfied to the point of threatening violence if they do not receive these compensations. However, since the operations in Petit Goäve and Terre Rouge, these elements have remained calm in the hope that they will receive money and jobs from the TGOH. The estimated 2,200 ExFadH are spread throughout the country, and are led by ex-Non-Commissioned Officers (NCOS) in different regions but have no national leader. As long as MINUSTAH is in the country and the ExFadH retain their hope of receiving compensation, they will not be a threat to the government.

The present security problem is criminal in nature and results from the illegal activities of the gangs in Port-au-Prince and its suburbs Cité Soleil and Bel Air. These gangs have different motivations: some act on their own initiative for their own benefit; others are involved with drug trafficking. Some gangs from Cité Soleil used to receive financial support from ex-President Aristide, but since his departure, they have resorted to other income sources such as carjacking and kidnapping. There is evidence to show that many disturbances and manifestations calling for the return of Aristide were organized and supported by these gangs, who also wanted to destabilize the TGOH. As long as MINUSTAH was in place, the gangs were unable to overthrow the TGOH; nonetheless, they created an intense atmosphere of insecurity. The security situation outside Port-au-Prince has been calm and the crime rate is more or less comparable to crime rates in other countries. Overall, however, there is chronic violence due to a general distrust of the HNP and a dysfunctional justice system. This has led some Haitians to take justice into their own hands, at times, to the point of lynching criminals.

Finally, due to the lack of running water, lack of food, and all too frequent natural disasters, the country exists in a state of ongoing human crisis, requiring the sustained help of the international community.

Mission des Nations Unies de Stabilisation en Haiti (MINUSTAH)

MINUSTAH is a complex peace "keeping" operation under Chapter VII of the UN Charter. In other words, it is not a traditional peacekeeping mission as described under Chapter VI, which implies the existence of a ceasefire between belligerent parties and the acceptance by those parties of UN troops to maintain peace. In Haiti, there was no ceasefire as such, since the ExFadH and the gangs did not agree to lay down their weapons. Hence, it would be more accurate to view MINUSTAH as a peace-enforcement mission. In fact, the US concept of a "Three-Block War" is most fitting here. In one block offensive actions are required such as the operations in Terre Rouge and Petit Goäve against the ExFadH or the operations in Cité Soleil and Bel Air against the gangs. The second block consists of more traditional peacekeeping or stability operations, which are conducted in most of the country. The final block refers to the distribution of humanitarian assistance by Mission's troops, in support of international aid agencies.

UN Security council resolution 1542 of 30 April 2004 provides MINUSTAH's Mission mandate, reflecting its multidimensional nature. The resolution also specifies that the Mission is acting under Chapter VII of the UN Charter. The three main objectives of the Mission are: to provide a secure and stable environment, to safeguard the respect for human rights, and to help the Haitian political process move forward. In order to fulfill these three objectives, MINUSTAH must carry out a number of tasks and activities in close co-operation and coordination with relevant Haitian authorities at the national, regional, and local levels.

The tasks in question can be grouped as follows:

Secure and stable environment tasks:
- To *support* the transitional government.
- To *assist* the transitional government in monitoring, restructuring and reforming the HNP.
- To *assist* with the restoration and maintenance of the rule of law, public safety and public order, through the provision inter alia of operational support to the HNP.
- To *protect* UN personnel, facilities, installations and equipment, and to ensure the security and freedom of movement of its personnel.
- To *protect* civilians under imminent threat of physical violence.

Human rights tasks:
- To *assist* the transitional government as well as Haitian human rights institutions and groups in their efforts.
- To *monitor and report* on the human rights situation.

Political process tasks:
- To *support* the constitutional and political process under way.
- To *assist* the transitional government in its efforts to bring about a process of dialogue and reconciliation.
- To *assist* the transitional government in its efforts to organize, monitor, and carry out free municipal, parliamentary and presidential elections.
- To *assist* the transitional government to extend state authority throughout Haiti and to support good governance at the local level.

As the introduction to this book indicates, Haiti has been referred to as a fragile or failing state. As is often the case with this type of state, its public institutions are largely dysfunctional. However, as indicated by the key words *"assist"* and *"support"* in the above list of tasks, MINUSTAH is neither the lead nor does it often possess the authority to execute these tasks on its own. Haiti is a sovereign state and MINUSTAH has a supportive role to play. This is the crux of the challenge; most of the Haitian institutions are dysfunctional and trying to assist or support these dysfunctional institutions is difficult, to say the least. In many instances MINUSTAH has had to take the lead or fill the vacuum, especially in the domain of security and stability.

To accomplish its tasks, MINUSTAH is organized as per figure 1 on pg. 78. The Special Representative of the Secretary General (SRSG) is the diplomat who directs all the United Nations components of the Mission. He has a small personal staff to help him deal with numerous political issues related to the international community and the TGOH. In addition to coordinating and managing all the elements of the Mission, he must deal with most of the daily crises which are mainly tactical in nature but have strategic or political consequences. It is my opinion that the headquarters at the Mission level lacks sufficient human resource personnel to assist the SRSG in commanding and controlling all the elements of the Mission.

Another key figure in the Mission is the Force Commander (FC). He is an Army lieutenant-general commanding a force of 7,400 soldiers from fifteen different countries, all with differing levels of professionalism and experience in dealing with the type of security tasks required in Haiti. Some contingents are less successful than others for a variety of reasons. For example, many of the initial contingents deployed to Haiti expected to perform more traditional Chapter VI peacekeeping tasks, and it has been difficult for some to understand, accept, and execute the offensive actions necessary to accomplish the mission, actions which are authorized under Chapter VII.

Still, MINUSTAH has successfully created a secure and stable environment throughout most of the country. A challenge remains in Cité Soleil, where Jordanian battalions recruited to secure the area, have yet to make much progress. This is due in part to their reluctance, and often refusal, to patrol the slums on foot, patrolling instead in armoured personnel carriers on the main streets only. This is not an effective way to control the difficult terrain of Cité Soleil, an area consisting almost exclusively of slums, and it continues to be Haiti's main security challenge.

The Principal Deputy of the SRSG (PDSRSG) is also a crucial Mission member since he is responsible for seven sections. The Admin section provides the logistic support to all the UN entities in the Mission, which is a tremendous task considering the limited indigenous Haitian capacity, the highly bureaucratic nature of UN processes, and the country's very poor infrastructure.

The Security section provides security for all UN civilian personnel and installations, and the Human Rights section, which is composed of a few individuals, is responsible for humanitarian related tasks. The Justice section, which has recently been established, will assist the TGOH in reforming the justice system. Due to a very slow deployment of its staff, almost no progress has been made in this area to date.

The UN Police (UNPOL) is seventeen hundred strong, and consists of officers from thirty-five different countries. The force is composed of two types of police officers: traditional street officers armed only with pistols, and eight Formed Police Units (FPU) of approximately one hundred officers each. These FPUS are equipped with assault rifles, riot control equipment, and armoured personnel carriers (APC). The street police officers' main tasks are to monitor and help reform the HNP while the FPUS are charged with security-related tasks similar to those carried out by the UN military forces. Like the military, the FPUS can do patrols, staff check points, and provide escorts and security to fixed installations (stability type tasks), but are not trained to carry out offensive actions on their own. They can, however, be asked to support military offensive operations against the gangs or ExFadHs, depending on the situation. The fact that the FPUS and military units are under the command and control of two different individuals (the Force Commander and the Police Commissioner) is problematic. The two forces perform similar security tasks in the same areas of responsibility, and despite the goodwill of all involved, this situation has created great challenges in terms of coordination. Indeed, it is a structure that goes against the well-proven principle of Unity of Command. A solution would be to place the FPUS under operational control of the military commanders in each area of responsibility, but this is a controversial issue, and, would require a change in policy at the UN headquarters in New York. However, it would increase efficiency and avoid potential involuntary fratricides (friendly fire incidents).

The Civil Affairs section is mandated to help build the government of Haiti's capacity to implement policy as well as improve public services at national, regional, and local or municipal levels. The Electoral section works with the Organization of American States (OAS) to assist the Conseil Electoral Provisoire (CEP) in organizing elections.

The Deputy SRSG (DSRSG) has two hats. First, he is the head of the in-country UN Development Program (UNDP), which has been in Haiti for many years. Second, he is in charge of the following MINUSTAH Sections: The Humanitarian Affairs section which coordinates UN and international humanitarian assistance; the Gender, Childhood and HIV/AIDS sections, which help in these respective fields and finally the DDR section, which assists with the Disarmament, Demobilization, and Reintegration (DDR) process. Finally the DSRSG coordinates the efforts of the other UN agencies in the country, such as the World Food Program.

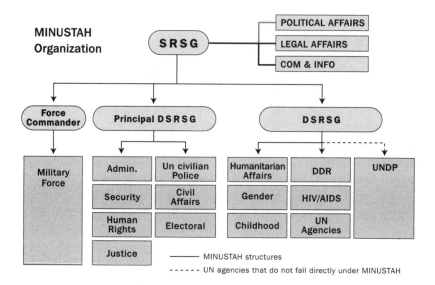

Figure 1: MINUSTAH Organizational Chart, 2005.

It is the large number of sections described above, coupled with their various objectives, that make MINUSTAH a truly multi-dimensional Mission, one which requires artful coordination. In fact, due to the lack of properly staffed headquarters at the Mission level, it became necessary for the military Chief of Staff, supported by the military planning staff, to chair a weekly coordination meeting, bringing together all the Mission sections, not a typical duty of a military Chief of Staff.

MINUSTAH's military mission can be summarized in the following way: "To ensure a secure and stable environment with the view of facilitating the political and human rights objectives of MINUSTAH." An assessment of MINUSTAH in the spring of 2005 determined that there was a lack of resources and authority to successfully carry out this mission. The UN Security Council Resolution

(UNSCR) 1608, dated 22 June 2005, authorized the deployment of one additional infantry battalion, the creation of a Sector HQ to command and control the troops in the Port-au-Prince area. It also increased the number of officers to UNPOL, and reaffirmed its authority to vet and certify officers in the HNP. This new UN resolution improved MINUSTAH's capability, increasing the Mission's capacity and efficiency. Nonetheless, in my opinion, it is still insufficient. The UNPOL should have been granted an "Executive Authority" which would have given the force the authority to arrest suspects. To date, UNPOL continues to be without this authority, forcing it to rely on the HNP to formally arrest criminals or corrupt police officers.

The main MINUSTAH internal difficulties have been and, in some instances, continue to be:

- The very slow deployment of troops to Haiti. It took more than a year to deploy the troops and this has contributed to the lack of law and order in some areas where there were no or not enough troops.
- The lack of a robust Mission Level HQ, which has resulted in poor coordination and direction among all the different agencies, as well as a lack of longer-term planning.
- The lack of reliable intelligence in support of operations. There is a need for Human Intelligence (HUMINT) and Signal Intelligence (SIGINT) to increase the efficiency of the operations aimed at the gangs and the corrupt elements of the HNP.
- Some of the troops lack Fighting in Build up Areas (FIBUA) skills to conduct offensive actions against the gangs in the slums of Port-au-Prince.
- The lack of Close Air Support (CAS), which would support offensive operations and help neutralize snipers on roofs, towers, and hills. MINUSTAH has suffered some casualties as a result of this deficiency.
- The ever-increasing demand and pressure associated with providing around-the-clock security for all types of UN, government, industrial, or electoral buildings. This demand consumes most of the troops, which consequently diminishes their ability to execute all the other security tasks.
- The UN Logistic system is too bureaucratic and unresponsive to the needs of a changing security and operational environment.

The Canadian Contribution to MINUSTAH

Canada initially sent a task force (TF) of approximately five hundred soldiers as part of the Multinational Interim Force (MIF) in the spring of 2004. This task force came under the command of the MINUSTAH Military Force once the latter replaced the MIF in June 2004. The Canadian task force remained in Haiti until July/August 2004 in order to facilitate the transition from the MIF to the MINUSTAH. At present, the Canadian Forces have one colonel (the Chief of Staff) and three majors on staff at the Military Force Headquarters. In addition Canada provides one hundred police officers to UNPOL from the Royal Canadian Mounted Police (RCMP) and a number of French-speaking police from Québec. The Police Commissioner is also a Canadian. Although the Canadian military and police force members are modest, they contribute sought-after expertise in key positions.

In summary, MINUSTAH is a complex Peace Support Operation Mission. This is a result of the precarious situation in Haiti, the structure of the mission with its numerous actors addressing multi-dimensional issues, and the demands of having to execute simultaneously what the Americans call the Three-Block War: humanitarian assistance, stabilization security tasks, and offensive operations. The Mission operates under Chapter VII of the UN Charter, which provides legal authority to use lethal force if necessary in offensive operations in order to enforce the mandate.

The country's lack of good governance at all levels is mainly attributable to the high levels of corruption within Haiti's state institutions. At the same time, it will take many years to reform and build the Haitian National Police to the point where it is able to ensure a secure and stable environment for Haitians. The DDR process, for its part, remains stalled due to the lack of government resolve and resources. Haiti needs massive economic development in order to provide employment for the population, which should diminish the incentive for crime and corruption.

Regrettably, the UN logistic system is too bureaucratic and not flexible enough to respond in a timely fashion to the needs of an evolving security situation requiring the redeployment of troops within the country. Moreover, MINUSTAH has found it difficult to win the information battle (prevent leaks) due to its internal public information deficiencies. The Mission also lacks close air support to assist its troops during offensive operations against the gangs. It is these gangs, which are found principally in Port-au-Prince, that currently constitute the main threat to security in Haiti. At the moment, the main threat is of a criminal nature, for example, the large number of kidnappings and the daily exchange of gunfire between the gangs and MINUSTAH in Cité Soleil. The rest of the country enjoys a relatively secure and stable environment, and, in spite of the many challenges outlined above, the Mission has made good progress.

Recommendations for Mission Success

My view is that the present mandate is inadequate since it will not create the conditions necessary to solve Haiti's problems in the longterm. To succeed, the international community must establish a UN protectorate or trusteeship, or, to be more politically correct, a transitional administration, for a period of ten to fifteen years. If the UN protectorate is not politically acceptable, the UN Security Council needs to give an "Executive Mandate" to UNPOL, essentially subordinating the Haitian National Police to UNPOL. Aristide's influence needs to be neutralized in order to undermine the Cité Soleil gangs' aspirations to see his return and their hope to regain some legitimacy and freedom of action. The United Nations must overcome its reluctance to provide troops with much needed intelligence, particularly tactical signal intelligence. And finally, the UN must provide proper Close Air Support to its troops in order to minimize casualties.

Building Haiti through Civil Society

6

The Role of the Private Sector and the Diaspora in Rebuilding Haiti

CARLO DADE

Extreme poverty and political instability have made Haiti a bellwether of changes in the practice of development and nation-building. Advances and trends less pronounced elsewhere in Latin America and the Caribbean are more visible in Haiti, bringing into sharp focus two of the most important recent changes in the reality and practice of development: the greater role of the private sector and the need for traditional development actors to respond to this new reality.

Globally, the private sector, which incorporates private individuals through remittances and private companies through social investments in public health, basic education, the environment and community development, is now the largest funder of direct poverty alleviation, if not actual development, in the developing world. Responding to this new reality and seizing the possibilities it offers will be crucial to success in the long-term mission to rebuild Haiti.

The Global Picture: Remittances

Remittances flowing to the developing world in 2005 were estimated to approach US$250 billion, or close to three times the estimated amount of all forms of Official Development Assistance (ODA) from all donors for the same year.[1] The narrow, official, definition of remittances is financial transfers sent by migrants and immigrants, or Diasporas,[2] to family and relatives in their communities of origin. These transfers may be to individuals for basic needs such as housing, health, and education or may be sent collectively and invested in community development projects. A broader, more useful, definition of remittances would include transfers and financial flows from other sectors, due solely to the emotional or familial ties that define Diasporas. Two examples of this would be receipts from telecommunications charges and from tourism. In the former case, national telephone companies in the developing world receive hundreds of millions of dollars from telecom transfer charges generated by telephone calls from the Diaspora to family members back home. In the latter case, a vivid example is that of Haitian tourism. Given the popular perception of the country the concept of Haitian tourism may seem at first to be an oxymoron, yet each year hundreds of thousands of people visit the country and pay airport taxes, visit restaurants, stay in hotels and spend money on goods and services. Haitians going home to Haiti are not the stereotypical image of a Caribbean tourist. The question is, are the receipts earned from their travel better considered as remittances or as normal tourist receipts?

There is a curious debate in the development community about the importance of remittances, centring on whether the funds are used for productive purposes, contributing to development, or whether they are simply used for "consumption" and do not contribute directly to development. The argument is curious for two reasons. First, it ignores the human capital improvement aspects of remittances. Money that is invested in food, housing, education and health improves the lives and productivity of those who consume and is therefore a productive investment. Second, remittances stimulate the local economies into which they flow. The result is similar to money entering a community from workers at a new factory. The increase in incomes of workers at the factory benefits local shopkeepers, service providers, and the local housing market and also triggers an increase in non-productive leisure consumption. A similar dynamic occurs when remittances enter a community. Yet, it is only in the case of remittances where the development community has considered that the increase in leisure consumption is a problem. Perhaps a better term than "curious" to describe the differing reactions of the development community to this phenomenon would be "paternalistic."

Remittances, when defined narrowly as financial transfers, have a huge impact on development and the potential to have a still larger impact as enablers of development. Not only used for direct poverty alleviation, these funds are also invested in education, health, housing, and micro-enterprise. Even where remittances do not build schools they make it possible for children to attend school; even where they do not build health clinics they make it possible for people to buy medicine and even where they do not create businesses they make it possible for people to invest in or sustain micro-businesses and farms. These transfers are a major source of liquidity and a potential source for capital in impoverished communities that are not, or at best poorly, served by formal sector financial institutions. As such, remittance flows have the potential to induce formal sector financial institutions to work with unbanked, or those without access to formal sector financial services, populations. Although the introduction of these financial flows into poor communities can create or perpetuate social and economic disparities, this is no different from what is seen in normal development interventions such as creating new jobs, building infrastructure, or investment.

Direct financial transfers from the Diaspora to family in their communities of origin are only one aspect of remittance flows. Equally important are collective remittances and non-financial remittances, such as skills and business opportunities. The rise in importance of collective and non-financial remittances is a direct result of the impact of accelerated globalization on migration.

Migration has become dominant as a feature of the developing world. In Latin America and the Caribbean, anywhere from 15 to 80 per cent of a country's population may reside abroad. For example, in the case of Jamaica, one-half of individuals who identify themselves as Jamaican, and who have some valid claim to citizenship, reside off island. In the case of Mexico, there are almost as many Mexicans residing in the United States, as there are Canadians in Canada.

Present-day migration differs significantly from migration from past periods in that migrants today are connected continuously, dynamically, and intimately to their communities of origin. This difference is due to technological advances, or what Manuel Orozco terms the four "Ts" of globalization, modern telecommunications, transportations, transfers (financial), and trade. Even though connections between migrants and their home communities existed in the past, modern technology has so drastically changed and enhanced their connections, that a new reality has been created.

In the past, one would speak of migrants and immigrants as figuratively having a foot in two places, two cultures at the same time. Today, that description is almost literal. Finances permitting, migrants can speak by cell phone or teleconference daily with family back home regardless of whether or not the participants are literate and regardless of whether they are in the capital or the countryside; they can read the same newspapers (often before people back home), watch the same news broadcasts, run the family finances (including paying bills and buying groceries), and return home at will on one of several scheduled daily flights. This constitutes a profound difference from earlier eras of migration, which often featured circular and return migration.

Migrants today continue to act and interact in their communities of origin on a (practically) real time basis. Ubiquitous, low-cost air travel and real-time personal communications did not exist with earlier waves of migration. This has changed how migrants interact with their home communities, created new possibilities for interaction, and has opened these possibilities to a wider section of the migrant community. In the past, one would speak of "return migration" as linking migrants to their communities of origin; today, in contrast, the Internet, coupled with affordable long-distance telephone service, makes it seem as if migrants never actually leave their home communities.

The four Ts mentioned above enable a vast and dynamic exchange of human capital, ideas, practices, and resources to flow through transnational networks. These exchanges play a role, and have the potential to play a larger role, in community development. A simple example is the financial contributions made by migrants to development projects in their home communities. For example, most groups now raise money through dances, lotteries, and football leagues to repair schools or to buy an ambulance. Through technological advances such as video and web cameras, migrants are able to see their projects develop in real time. Through enhanced electronic financial transfer mechanisms, migrants are able to move more money more easily, to more remote locations to fund these projects. And through rapid and increasingly affordable transportation, migrants are able to return home more frequently to participate in these projects.

Collective remittances are one manifestation of this enhanced connectivity. Collective remittances are funds that are pooled by members of the Diaspora, most often through clubs, associations, football teams and churches. In this instance, membership consists of people from the same village, district or city. These collective funds are invested in community development projects such as repairing the local church, school, health clinic or irrigation system. In several countries such as Mexico and El Salvador the federal and municipal governments have programs to facilitate and match these investments.[3]

Non-financial transfers such as knowledge, skills, new social practices, and business opportunities, though less well-studied, also play a significant role in promoting development in countries with high out-migration. Though not remittances in the technical, financial definition, these transfers flow along the same transnational channels as financial remittances; that is, they are transferred by telecommunications and personal interaction through travel. As they apply to development, non-financial transfers greatly impact political and social development when Diasporas agitate for changes in local government such as greater accountability, transparency, and more participation, based on their experiences with governments outside their community of origin. We can see this trend in the agricultural sector as well, when agricultural migrants return to rural communities with new farming technology. The money these migrants earn abroad also allows them to purchase or duplicate new technologies for use on farms in their home communities. There is one well-documented case of such a transfer of technology leading to an agricultural revival in the state of Zacatecas in Mexico.[4] Recent research has also pointed to the role of knowledge transfer by the Indian Diaspora in sparking the high-tech boom in India and in facilitating foreign investment.

The Global Picture: Private Companies

Similar quantitative data is not readily available for the direct contributions made by the private sector. Anecdotally, we know that private companies are increasingly investing financial and human resources to support the communities in which they operate. The private sector is expanding their role beyond charity and philanthropy, and taking an active role in supporting basic health and education programs as well as environmental initiatives through external Corporate Social Responsibility (CSR) programs. A recent survey by the Canadian Foundation for the Americas (FOCAL) of CSR spending by Canadian companies in Guatemala, Chile, and Trinidad and Tobago found that Canadian companies in these countries are spending approximately 20 per cent of what the Canadian International Development Agency (CIDA) is spending on basic development projects.[5] The United States Agency for International Development (USAID) estimates that US corporations contribute approximately US$2.8 billion per year to support development projects outside of the US.[6] In addition, companies based in the developing world have begun to play a more active role in supporting local community development, and companies throughout the Americas such as Arcor and Minetti in Argentina, Boticário and Poemar in Brazil, E Leon Jimenez and Helados Bon, in the Dominican Republic, and countless others, have invested hundreds of millions of dollars to finance and carry out local community development projects.

The Case of Haiti in Particular

Although many in the international development community have always known or suspected that the private sector, both individuals and companies, contributed to development, it has only been in the last few years that the magnitude and scope of these contributions have been understood. The international development community is struggling to learn how best to work with these "new" actors.

In Haiti, due to the de facto lack of a functioning state and the manifest deficiency of traditional development actors, this struggle to integrate private companies and the Haitian Diaspora is even more crucial. Analyzing the failures of traditional development actors and strategies is a long and complicated task and it is not the purpose of this chapter. However, what is clear is that there has been a lack of progress in improving the basic conditions of life and in creating an enabling environment for private sector growth. Business and the Diaspora have been forced to step into the vacuum of failure left by traditional development actors and their strategies. It is highly doubtful that the private sector and the Diaspora can replace traditional development agencies. However, they are making important contributions and bringing new resources, energy, and innovation to the development project. It is crucial that traditional development agencies determine how best to facilitate and incorporate these contributions. While the Diaspora and private enterprises have done much to keep the floor from falling out beneath Haiti, allowing people to survive, making these contributions take on a transformative role will require action by traditional development actors.

The Contributions of Haiti's Private Sector

In the case of the Diaspora, the Inter-American Development Bank (IDB) estimates that over US$1 billion was sent to Haiti by those living outside of the country. This figure equates to roughly one-quarter of the country's Gross Domestic Product (GDP) and is over four times the Organization of Economic Co-operation and Development (OECD) figures for all forms of Official Development Assistance (ODA). In 2002, remittances were more than six times greater than ODA. In short, the Diaspora have been sending four to six times more money to Haiti than has the governments of the United States, France, Canada, and the Inter-American Development Bank, the World Bank, the European Union, and the United Nations combined. And, unlike much donor funding, money from the Diaspora is given, not loaned, and therefore imposes no future financial obligations on the government of Haiti.

Figures on collective remittances to Haiti are more difficult to obtain, but two sources provide an indication of likely scope. The Regroupement des organismes canado-haïtiens pour le développement (ROCAHD) based in Montréal, Canada, is a federation of Haitian Hometown Associations (HTA) that, in partnership with CIDA, work together to fund small-scale community development projects in members' home communities in Haiti.[7] In 2003, the last year in which published reports are available, ROCAHD raised CA$118,342 for development projects in Haiti.[8] These funds supported approximately eight major projects, which are defined as being larger than CA$5,000 and smaller, direct access projects, defined as less than CA$3,000 each. Based on interviews conducted in 2005 with a range of Haitian organizations in Canada, it appears that ROCAHD contributions represent close to 90 per cent of what is sent from Canada to Haiti as collective remittances. This means that roughly CA$11,800 sent by other organizations that are not members of ROCAHD and that the total amount of collective remittances is approximately CA$130,000 per year. Unfortunately, there is no accurate data for the amount of individual remittances from Canada, but the IDB estimates that Canada accounts for approximately 10 per cent of remittance flows to countries in Latin America and the Caribbean. In the case of Haiti this would equate to US$100 million dollars or CA$116 million dollars, meaning that the collective remittances represent only about one-tenth of 1 per cent of the entire flow of remittances from Canada.

In addition to ROCAHD, there are several other Haitian HTA federations in Canada and countless more HTAS in the United States. One of the largest Haitian HTA federations in the US, with thirty-seven members is the Fédération des Associations Régionales Étrangères (FARE) located in Brooklyn, New York. Less information is available about Haitian HTA federations in the US due to the lack of official partnerships with development agencies and the attendant lack of publicly available documentation, such as annual reports. However, based on interviews with FARE members conducted in 2002 and 2003, the average amount spent per year per organization on projects in its home community in Haiti was reported to be US$10,000. While this amount is several times higher than that reported by Haitian HTAS in Canada, it is not an implausible figure. In general, Haitian HTAS in New York appeared to be wealthier, larger, and able to raise more funds than their counterparts in Canada. This also would track differences in per capita income between Canada and the US.[9] It must be stressed though that this analysis is based on a limited set of observations and more research is needed.

Non-financial flows to Haiti are even more difficult to track and quantify than collective remittances. However, these flows have had an important impact on development in Haiti. One important contribution has been the recruitment of members of the Diaspora by development agencies. A leader in this area has been the quasi-official development agency of the state of Florida, the Florida Association for Volunteer Action in the Caribbean and the Americas (FAVACA), which has placed countless volunteers from Florida's large Haitian community in short-term assignments in Haiti. FAVACA has also worked with USAID to engage the Haitian Diaspora in creating a demand for Haitian produce in Florida's supermarkets and stores. Efforts to encourage members of the Diaspora to return to Haiti have been advanced by the United Nations in its recruitment of technical advisors to Haiti's provisional government. In fact, members of the Diaspora are currently in important leadership and cabinet positions.

Another aspect of Diaspora contributions is seen in foreign direct investment. In 2003, a group of wealthy Haitians from the Diaspora joined with prominent members of the Haitian business community to form PromoCapital, an investment fund to identify, structure, and promote investments by the Diaspora in Haiti. The fund has sold over 400,000 shares to sixty-seven shareholders split roughly between Haitian investors residing in Haiti and in the Diaspora. The fund has raised US$1 million to focus on large investments such as infrastructure, real estate, and export-oriented production. The fund also will be able take positions in public offerings of state-owned enterprises and infrastructure projects carried out under the reconstruction programs for Haiti being administered by international donors. Though Foreign Direct Investment (FDI) is not often included under remittances, in the case of Haiti, the difficulty of the government and international donors in attracting FDI to the country should prompt a re-evaluation of this tendency. Clearly, in Haiti there are opportunities to achieve a return on foreign investment. But foreign firms have not pursued these opportunities.[10] Diasporas are understood to posses certain knowledge advantages that facilitate their ability to invest in their home communities and give them advantages over non-Diaspora foreign investors.[11] In Haiti, as is likely the case in other fragile states where there is large Diaspora-driven FDI, this investment seems to stem from something other than knowledge advantage. There appears to be an emotional connection and a sense of obligation driving the investment, though the emotional connection does not appear to override the discipline of the profit motif. However, if the primary driver for the investment decision is an emotional connection rather than maximizing return on investment, one has to wonder if this form of transfer is better considered a remittance, a transfer based on an obligation and connection to one's home community, or whether it is simply another form of Foreign Direct Investment.

The role of the private sector in supporting development differs from what is seen elsewhere in Latin America and the Caribbean because of extremely low foreign investment and the relatively small size of Haitian companies. As a result, the large scale Corporate Social Responsibility (CSR) and community investment projects seen elsewhere in the region, such as those funded by Falconbridge Mining in the neighbouring Dominican Republic do not exist in Haiti. However, as in many parts of the developing world, the Haitian private sector has been forced to fill in for a state that lacks the institutional capacity, tax base, fiscal indiscipline, and personnel to provide basic social services. In response, the private sector has provided its own basic services in areas such as security and transportation. Beyond these obvious areas of intervention, many firms in Haiti undertake activities related to public goods, such as support for education, public health, and community infrastructure, by quietly funding transportation, basic health care and supporting local schools.

One exception has been in the area of public health where the SogeBank Foundation, the philanthropic arm of the country's largest bank, administers the largest HIV/AIDS prevention project in the country using a US$24.4 million grant from the Global Fund to Fight AIDS, Tuberculosis and Malaria. The SogeBank foundation overseeing provision of antiretroviral therapy to more than twelve hundred people with HIV and provides a massive gamut of prevention services targeting youth that are scheduled to reach over four hundred thousand Haitians. In choosing the SogeFoundation to run the project, the Global Fund had to contend with opposition from the then ruling *Lavalas* government as well as traditional development actors. The Fund argued, however, that the only entity in Haiti with the managerial capacity to administer the grant, ensure transparency, and produce results was the SogeBank Foundation. This aspect of the project has received negligible mention in reviews and discussions of the project by international health agencies and traditional aid agencies. Yet, given the history of corruption and failed development projects and the fact that the Fund has terminated grants to Myanmar and Uganda, the involvement of the SogeBank Foundation and its ability to manage the program is as important as the technical capabilities of partnering NGOs.[12]

In October 2005, seventeen leaders of the Haitian private sector held a historic and unprecedented meeting in Canada with then IDB president Enrique Iglesias to discuss the desire of the private sector to emerge from behind the scenes and to take a more active and public role in the rebuilding of Haiti. The meeting was neither a gripe session by private sector actors unhappy with the pace of disbursements or development policies nor was it a request for funding for pet projects. Instead the meeting was more of a coming-out event for the private sector, which demonstrated itself to be the one sector in Haiti with the skills and capacity to contribute to large-scale change and improvements in the economy and living conditions.

Interestingly, the meeting began with the private sector calling for a "revolution of growth" in Haiti. Representatives suggested encouraging private sector growth in order to stimulate growth, increase access to capital, improve security through lessening social tensions over income disparity and lack of economic growth and expand the tax base. This was acknowledged as being a response to the failure of the neo-liberal agenda elsewhere. The private sector participants at the meeting stated openly that one of their top priorities was to ensure that more Haitians benefited from economic growth, and that access to opportunity be greatly expanded in order to ensure widespread support for a market-based economy, trade, and investment. Beyond rhetoric, the private sector participants presented concrete ideas and plans for bringing this about by promoting land titling and increasing access to credit for people in the informal sector.

Other ideas put forth included the creation of public/private boards to oversee the management of crucial government services, and private sector advisory boards to assist the government in economic planning and budgeting. The private sector and donors attending the meeting acknowledged that the private sector is the only agent in Haiti with the expertise and technical capacity to effectively carry out many "government" tasks. At the same time, there was uniform agreement that the private sector could not replace the government and that current interventions could only serve as transition measures until the government gained the capacity and competence to take on its traditional responsibilities. Beyond these areas, the private sector put forth a number of ideas that are available in the conference report.[13]

Perhaps the most important result of the meeting was that CIDA and the IDB modified their position on the private sector's role. Neither agency had developed a clear idea of how the private sector might contribute to Haiti's development. To a large degree, the same was true regarding the Diaspora. A December 2004 meeting on the role of the Haitian Diaspora in supporting Haiti's new development and reconstruction plan, the Interim Cooperation Framework (ICF), was convened in Montreal by the Canadian government, with Diaspora representatives from Canada, the United States, and France in attendance. While most bi- and multi-lateral agencies were aware of the fact that Diaspora groups worked in Haiti, they had not fully grasped the vast scope of their activities, the large number of groups involved, or the depth of their commitment to the country.

As a result of these two meetings, the international development community has created space for the increased formal participation of the private sector and the Diaspora in the multi-donor framework for rebuilding Haiti.

In fact, members of the Haitian private sector who met in Canada with the IDB president were invited to a crucial donors' meeting on the ICF, which was held in Brussels in December 2005. Moreover, space has been created to ensure that future consultations will include participation from the Diaspora.

The Future

So where do donors go from here? Working with the Diaspora and the private sector poses unique challenges for traditional development actors such as multilateral development banks and bilateral aid agencies. Neither Diaspora organizations nor private companies are professional development actors. In the Haitian case, both sets of actors will require capacity-building and institutional strengthening. In the case of the Diaspora these investments will exceed what is normally provided by development agencies to traditional NGO partners as is illustrated by the case of ROCAHD, whose apprenticeship, funded by CIDA, lasted seven years. The largest impediment to working more closely with the private sector, however, will be overcoming perceptions and attitudes within development agencies where there is a widespread distrust of the private sector and a tendency to view it as a problem rather than as a potential solution, let alone a potential partner.

A related problem has been, and will continue to be, the ability of development agencies to partner with these groups. Both the private sector and the Diaspora have been accustomed to managing their own funds and running their own programs. Despite rhetoric on consultation and responsive development, traditional development agencies prefer to design and oversee programs, allowing their partners to implement a predetermined set of plans. Indeed, the first reaction in the development community to the "discovery" of billions of dollars of remittances was an attempt to determine how these resources might be "channelled" to "productive uses." This of course assumed that the channeller was a better judge of how remittances should be used. It also presumed that the priorities of the channeller should take precedence over those of the sender. Fortunately, this initial euphoria was quickly dispelled.[14] However, the fact that this line of thinking developed at all illustrates the nature of the relationship between Diasporas and development agencies.

These recent experiences of USAID, CIDA and the IDB show that it is possible to work with the private sector and the Diaspora. What is needed now is a commitment to move beyond the occasional and isolated project. Past experience needs to be examined in order to develop more comprehensive and unified approaches leading to more dynamic and sustainable forms of engagement and partnership. And, as should be clear from the problematical attempts to quantify Diaspora and private sector participation, more rigorous research is clearly needed on these issues, especially in Canada.

Notes

1 Remittance estimates include a 50 per cent adjustment for estimated unreported transfers. These figures come from The World Bank, *Global Economic Prospects 2006* (Washington, DC: World Bank, 2006). ODA estimates are from a Statement by Mr. Richard Manning, Chairman. World Bank, "OECD Development Assistance Committee (DAC) Development Committee Meeting," DC/S/2005–0064 (Washington, DC: World Bank, 25 September 2005).

2 The term Diaspora is now used to refer to the entirety of people who reside in one location but identify themselves, wholly or partially based on their origin in, or connection to, another location. The term encompasses migrants, first, second, and even third generation immigrants, expatriates, students and seasonal workers.

3 An excellent discussion of the development role of collective remittances may be found in Sarah Gammage, "Crowding in Collective Remittances: Lessons Learned from State-HTA Collaborations in El Salvador," unpublished paper.

4 Sandra Nichols, "Mexican Migration and Transfer of Agricultural Innovations," paper prepared for presentation at: Asociación Mexicana de Estudios Rurales Cuarto Congreso, Morelia, Michoacán, California Institute for Rural Studies, 20–23 June 2003.

5 Carlo Dade, "External CSR Practice and Investments by Canadian Corporations in Latin America and the Caribbean" (Ottawa: Canadian Foundation for the Americas, September 2005).

6 USAID, "Foreign Aid In The National Interest: Promoting Freedom, Security, And Opportunity" (Washington, DC: USAID, 2002).

7 ROCAHD was created in 1987, when Haitian HTAS in Montreal that had been funding small-scale projects in Haiti began to apply to CIDA for money that was made available following the fall of the Duvalier dictatorship in 1986. CIDA was unable to afford the transaction costs of financing small projects with individual HTAS so it suggested that these associations come together to coordinate their efforts and projects. In response to the CIDA request, a group of Haitian HTAS began working under the umbrella of the Association québécoise des organismes de coopération internationale (ACOCQI), a pre-existing Quebecois group that did international development work with CIDA. CIDA financed ROCAHD's internship with ACOC for seven years at which point, in 1994, the Haitian associations were able to take over management of the relationship from ACOCQI and found their own federation, ROCAHD. This information is based on interviews with ROCAHD, carried out in 2001 by Margarita Mooney, PhD candidate at Princeton University for the Inter-American Foundation, and by the author in 2005.

8 ROCAHD also received CA$416,740 in matching funds from CIDA and the Ministère des Relations Internationales du Québec. See, Regroupement des organismes canado-haïtiens pour le développement, *Rapport Annuel 2003–2004* (Montreal, Canada 2004).

9   See for example, Centre for the Study of Living Standards, "The Canada-US Income Gap," (Ottawa: June 2000). According to CSLS, at the end of the 1990s, per capita income in Canada had dropped to about 78 per cent of per capita income in the US.

10 This information comes from interviews conducted in Port-au-Prince in the summer of 2005 with representatives from the Inter-American Development Bank in Haiti and several members of the Haitian business community.

11 See for example, V.N. Balasubramanyam and Yingqi Wei, "The Diaspora and Development," Working Paper, (Lancaster, UK: Lancaster University Department of Economics, 31 March 2003).

12 The "success" of the SogeFoundation administration in Haiti deserves a note of caution. The grants in Haiti are not performing as well as similar grants in other countries. Of the four grants in operation all are behind by at least five months in their implementation schedule and one is behind by close to one year. For relative grant performance statistics see <www.aidspan.org>. As reported in the *AfricaFocus Bulletin* on 9 November 2005, other than Uganda and Myanmar, the Global Fund has shown an unwillingness to terminate grants even when faced with evidence of lack of performance or fraud.

13 The Canadian Foundation for the Americas, "The Role of the Private Sector in Rebuilding Haiti: Dialogue Document from a Roundtable" held Friday 9 September—Saturday 10 September 2005 at Meech Lake, Québec, Canada (Ottawa: FOCAL, 2005).

14 An important step in this regard was a report issued from a conference on remittances and development convened by the Inter-American Foundation, the World Bank and the UN Economic Commission for Latin America and the Caribbean, held in Washington, DC, in March of 2001. See, Inter-American Foundation, "Approaches to Increasing the Productive Value of Remittances," (Washington, DC, 2001).

7

Dissonant Voices
Northern NGO and Haitian Partner
Perspectives on the Future of Haiti

JIM HODGSON

This chapter reflects on how the United Church of Canada has cautiously and delicately managed its relationships with Haitian partners, exploring the various perspectives of its development partners and the difficulties associated with supporting them in a constantly shifting and uncertain political context.

The United Church of Canada is the country's largest Protestant denomination with approximately 3,600 congregations across the country and close to three million people who identify the United Church as their religion. It maintains a large program of resource-sharing with other churches and non-governmental organizations (NGOs) around the world and has formed partnerships with about forty groups in close to a dozen countries in the Caribbean and Central America, plus Colombia. One part of its work is to discern from partner voices some perspectives that the Church can take into its regular conversations with the Canadian government, into its education efforts, and into those international spaces where it might have access.

Partners in Haiti

In Haiti, the United Church funds two partners. The first is the Methodist Church of Haiti, which is a district of the region-wide Methodist Church of the Caribbean and the Americas. This church has a substantial development program with a strong focus on the rural economy, including a micro-credit program that primarily benefits women who are market vendors, artisans and small farmers. This work receives modest support from the Canadian International Development Agency (CIDA) through its Canadian Partnership Branch co-financing agreement with the Church. The second partner is the Karl Lévêque Cultural Institute (ICKL),[1] a small NGO that works among grassroots organizations to promote reflection and analysis through popular education. Both partners emphasize the vital role of people who live in rural communities in determining the future of Haiti. The United Church also takes very seriously the perspectives of its regional ecumenical partner, the Caribbean Conference of Churches.

These partners do not share a single perspective on events in Haiti, a situation that I believe holds true for other churches and NGOs that support work in Haiti. Indeed, conversations with partners and colleagues in the country reveal three positions that should be taken seriously today and in the years ahead as new political options emerge.

The first position supports the various coalition efforts that emerged between 2000 and 2004, the best-known being the Group of 184 (G-184) coalition of civil society and business organizations.[2] In the two years prior to the departure of President Jean-Bertrand Aristide, these groups attained a good degree of consensus about the shape of a post-Aristide Haiti. It is worth noting that in the days immediately prior to the president's departure, many of them failed to denounce the violence committed by thugs who had links to previous dictatorships (individuals who had been associated with the with paramilitary Front pour l'Avancement et le Progrès Haïtien (FRAPH) militia during the 1990s, such as Louis Jodel Chamblain, as well as Guy Philippe, a former military officer standout). Since then, certain church colleagues, who either privately or publicly supported the G-184, have expressed a sense of marginalization. The interim government, according to these partners, has ignored their input and the consensus which they developed about the Haiti's future. Consequently, over the course of the 2005 electoral campaign, supporters of the G-184 and related groups have dispersed into a variety of camps.

The second position evident among the Church's partners is that of the grassroots movements that continue to support Aristide but are not linked to *chimères*, drug-traffickers, or urban street gangs. They include a network of independent Protestant churches and some Roman Catholic-based communities. Although these groups have been weakened since the end of the Aristide government, it is important to take their perspectives into account if a new progressive consensus is to emerge.

These groups argue that, based on the experience of the three successive presidential elections and their aftermath, the vote of Haiti's poor will never be respected by the Haitian elite or the international community. As evidence, they cite the 1991 military coup that interrupted Aristide's first administration, the international community's decision to suspend aid to Haiti during the administration of his successor, René Préval, because of fraudulent elections, and the refusal to restore aid after Aristide was re-elected in 2000. They trace this stance across Haitian history, from the international community's boycott of the country through most of the nineteenth century to the refusal to support Haiti's electoral choices over the past fifteen years.[3] These groups also support Aristide's demand for reparations from France, believing that France extracted unjust and excessive compensation from Haiti after the country gained independence in 1804. France has refused to pay these reparations and the demand has yet to be taken up by other political groups.

These partners are also profoundly disappointed by what they view as the Canadian government's "abandonment" of Aristide, not to mention Haitian constitutional democracy, in the days before 29 February 2004. They are also frustrated by Canada's failure to support the Caribbean governments that had pressed for a negotiated settlement over the course of the crisis. Those who have adopted this position also tend to disregard the human rights abuses (such as the assassination of radio journalist Jean Dominique in 2000) that occurred under Préval and Aristide's watch. They also overlook the corruption, drug-trafficking, the imposition of structural adjustment, the failure to implement progressive economic and social policies, and Aristide's own role in weakening Préval's government.

The third distinguishable position among partners is that of the grassroots organizations, journalists, and human rights groups that broke away from Aristide's *Lavalas* movement over the course of the last decade, or since Aristide was returned to power in 1994. Some abandoned the movement quite recently, after students and staff at the State University of Haiti were attacked by police in December 2003. According to these individuals, Aristide broke faith with the popular sectors that swept him into power in 1990 and returned him to office in 1994 and 2000. Moreover, they criticize Aristide for abandoning the political project that had once united Haiti's poor. They accept the intervention by international forces and the presence of foreign soldiers on Haitian soil as the price to be paid for ridding the country of a dangerous dictator, one whose armed supporters have persecuted them. According to these people, organizing an alternative popular project while Aristide remained in power was not possible.

This third view is rooted in the space that Aristide has occupied in Haitian popular imagination and culture. "Pe Titid," forever a priest in this mindset, has been a shrewd manipulator of popular language (Lavalas as a cleansing, furious flood) and symbols (the rooster as his political sign). According to this perspective, Aristide, through his domination of the public imagination and cultural space, created false hope, or a sort of false consciousness, that prevented peasant farmers from recognizing their condition as "peasants" and workers from recognizing their condition as "workers." Aristide's presence made it exceedingly difficult to demonstrate to poor urban and rural Haitians that he no longer defended their interests. For these people, the twenty years of *dechoukaj* (uprooting) since the end of the Duvalier dictatorship in 1986 generated an important lesson: popular movements and civil society organizations should maintain their autonomy from political parties and resist being co-opted by charismatic politicians. For the moment, it is difficult to imagine the groups that have adopted the second and third positions uniting around a common and new political project. But over time, I believe their class and social justice interests will draw them together again.

Foreign governments and national elites, for their part, are negotiating a new power structure that they imagine will guarantee their power. They seek the emergence of a state like that of El Salvador, where the electorate always makes the "right" choice, or the Dominican Republic, where it no longer matters which party is elected since all three parties implement the same neo-liberal project. Haiti's so-called friends seek conditions favourable to foreign capital: a docile, low-pay labour force, a compliant state, and a minimal security apparatus that is capable of little more than deterring a flood of migrants or illegal drugs.

A critical and valuable role for churches, non-governmental organizations, and even the Canadian government would be to create spaces for dialogue and collaboration among those whom the recent past has divided.

Partners in Canada

In Canada, the United Church frequently works in coalitions or less formal groups on policy questions that arise from its work with partners. On many issues of social justice and peace, it works with a coalition of Canadian churches known as KAIROS (Canadian Ecumenical Justice Initiatives), the Canadian Council of Churches, and Project Ploughshares. On international issues where questions of Canadian public policy come into play, the United Church also collaborates with the Canadian Council for International Cooperation (CCIC), as well as its various regional or thematic working groups. Outside Canada, it usually works within global or regional ecumenical structures, such as the World Council of Churches and the Caribbean Conference of Churches.

One of the challenges associated with responding to events in Haiti has been sifting through the widely divergent interpretations of what, in other contexts, might be accepted as basic facts. For instance, the simple matter of how many people voted in the November 2000 presidential election continues to be disputed. Phrases like "the opposition" and references to the "flawed elections in 2000" and apparent "facts and figures" related to these elections need to be carefully examined by journalists, as well as national and foreign NGOs and human rights groups, given their contested nature.

Aristide supporters believe he won the 26 November 2000 election with 90 per cent of the vote; Canadian columnist Rick Salutin cited this figure in his *Globe and Mail* column on 4 March 2005. At the same time, Aristide's opponents challenge these numbers, citing a low voter turnout number. For instance, US solidarity groups such as Pax Christi and Witness for Peace quote the official electoral council voter turnout figure of 60.5 per cent.[4] Further, opposition parties, most of which boycotted the election, use a whole other set of figures, citing numbers as low as 5 to 15 per cent. Haiti's private radio stations (usually controlled by the wealthy elite) cite similar figures, as do some foreign media. While Canada refused to send official observers to these elections, the head of the Caribbean Community monitoring mission, former St. Lucia Premier John Compton, estimated that the turnout had been about 15 to 20 per cent.[5]

These various figures have since been used to advance political positions. Those who cite the low turnout number question the legitimacy of the second Aristide presidency. Indeed, some cite the "flawed elections in 2000" as justification for the 2004 intervention. Conversely, those who cite the higher voter turnout number use this figure to validate Aristide's presidency. Put simply, they argue he was democratically elected and should be returned to office.

The senate elections that took place prior to the presidential elections are plagued with even greater controversy. Indeed, the opposition boycotted the November Presidential vote because of a dispute over the May 2004 senate elections; although some suggest the boycott was more strategic given that the opposition knew it could not have won against Aristide.[6] The May election dispute came about because the electoral council validated the victories of eight Lavalas candidates for seats in the senate when those candidates had failed to win an absolute majority (more than 50 per cent of votes cast). The opposition argued that run-off elections should have followed. Eventually, due to pressure from the Organization of American States (OAS), Aristide persuaded seven of the eight senators to resign and accepted OAS and Caribbean Community proposals for new elections. The opposition was not moved by this option and continued to demand Aristide's resignation. They dismissed the OAS-Caribbean Community-brokered negotiations as attempts to maintain the corrupt regime in power. The result was a political impasse that continued through to the February 2004 intervention.

Meanwhile, some Aristide supporters have attempted to diminish the importance of the disputed senate seats. For example, Canadian journalist Anthony Fenton was at best disingenuous when he dismissed the irregularities saying they affected only "seven out of seven thousand seats that were disputed." (He made the comment in an interview with Denis Paradis, the Chrétien-era Secretary of State for Latin America, Africa and La Francophonie.)[7] What Fenton fails to note, however, is that these were seven out of eight Senate seats, and that those victories would have awarded Aristide all but one of the thirty-two seats in the senate. Of course, even if all seven seats had been awarded to the opposition, Aristide would still have had more than three-quarters of the senate's seats.

What is important here is that fundamental differences over key issues have made it difficult for groups to forge alliances and agree on the essential elements of an advocacy strategy. Conflicting interpretations of events have divided those inside the country as well those abroad who seek to be in solidarity with the Haitian people. For instance, it is interesting to note that the foreign NGOs who defend human rights in Colombia, also tend to support the landless people's movement in Brazil and critique the US embargo on Cuba. However, on Haiti, these same groups and individuals find themselves in disagreement. Indeed, François l'Écuyer of the Montreal development organization Alternatives argues that the differing interpretations of events in Haiti have become the debate that divides the left.[8]

Despite these differences and after a close examination of all sides, the coalition with which the United Church has the greatest affinity is the Concertation pour Haïti. The Concertation is a Montreal-based grouping of twelve Québécois solidarity, development, labour, and human rights organizations that includes two church groups: the Canadian Catholic Organization for Development and Peace and Entraide Missionnaire. Regrettably, certain journalists on weblogs have suggested that the Concertation and its members' positions on Haiti have been shaped by the funding they receive from the Canadian government.[9] Concertation's positions on issues, however, are firmly rooted in the perspectives of its partners and in its long history of solidarity with the people of Haiti.

At the core of these debates and differences is the question: "To whom do we choose to listen?" Some of those associated with the Canadian NGO com-

munity have apparently chosen to use Haiti to advance a critique of US imperial ambitions in the hemisphere. While the "Empire" analysis is one with
which, at least in broad strokes, I essentially agree, those who apply it to Haiti
are failing to hear the voices of many Haitians with a very different reading of
the current situation. Clearly, much of what happened in Haiti before and
after February 2004 happened because the United States and its allies sought
particular outcomes related to their interests. Washington wants to curb the
flow of Haitian refugees. It also wants to eliminate drug shipments through
Haiti. Finally, Washington would like to see a compliant neo-liberal state that
protects foreign investors and guarantees low wages. Still, criticism of the
intervention, denunciation of the interim government's poor human rights
record and its disappointing failure to reform police, judicial, and penal systems should not automatically lead one to conclude that Aristide should be
returned to power. The anti-imperialist discourse needs to go deeper, and
above all, its proponents need to take seriously the voices of Haitians.

In the immediate aftermath of Aristide's departure, the United Church sent
a letter to Canada's then minister of foreign affairs, Bill Graham.[10] Bearing in
mind the varied perspectives of partners in Haiti and across the Caribbean
region, the letter tried to situate the 29 February 2004 intervention within the
context of a broader failure by Haiti's "friends" to provide solid, long-term
assistance to the country following Aristide's restoration to power in 1994.
The United Church questioned the military intervention without condemn-
ing it. It also shared the disappointment of its Caribbean partners that their
governments' diplomatic efforts had been pushed to the sidelines during the
crisis. Finally, the letter called for long-term collaboration with any new transition government.

There is a recent positive example of what is possible when people who
profess solidarity carefully listen to, and consider, a variety of voices. In April
2005, a delegation of peace activists toured Haiti and proclaimed:

> We recognize and salute the deep struggle of the Haitian people who have
> resisted, over the more than two hundred years following on their inde-
> pendence, the onslaughts, external and internal, that have opposed and
> posed obstacles to every advance of constructive popular forces. In that
> context, it seems important to us to highlight the fact that the departure
> of Aristide from the presidency and the country should be interpreted in
> the light of the growing social mobilization that had coalesced around the
> clamour for his resignation and was proposing its own transitional alter-
> natives.[11]

The delegation was organized by the Jubilee South coalition that advocates can-celling the foreign debts that strangle the aspirations of people in low-income countries and undermine the international community's laudable but insuf-ficient development goals. It was headed by the Nobel Peace Prize laureate Adolfo Pérez Esquivel and included people from South American countries that have contributed soldiers to the Mission des Nations Unies pour la sta-bilisation en Haïti (MINUSTAH).

This delegation might have been expected to echo the anti-imperialist voices in Canada that view the Haitian intervention in the same light as the wrong-headed intervention in Iraq. But instead its members listened to the voices of Haitians who continue to work for justice and peace. Although the delegation called for MINUSTAH's withdrawal, which may not be realistic at the moment, it did so in the context of an appeal to look at Haiti, not as a security problem, but rather in terms of its development needs. The security problems themselves may best be addressed by a thorough reform of the police, judicial, and penal systems, rather than long-term maintenance of the UN force. This perspective was repeated by Marc Arthur Fils-Aimé of the Karl Lévêque Cultural Institute, one of the United Church's partners in Haiti, when he spoke at the third Peoples Summit in Mar del Plata, Argentina: "Haiti needs assistance that will transform the lives of its poorest citizens, but emphasis on security and the presence of foreign troops will not help the popular sec-tors."[12] This comment brings us to a critical reflection on Canada's role in Haiti.

Canada and the 3-D Approach: Diplomacy, Defence, and Development

The United Church of Canada and its ecumenical and NGO colleagues agree that the world's myriad of problems require whole-of-government, multi-dimensional solutions. At the same time, Canada's 2005 International Policy Statement (IPS), a solid description of current policy directions, has been critiqued on several fronts by the Canadian Council for International Cooperation (CCIC), KAIROS and Project Ploughshares. The CCIC describes "important steps towards a progressive foreign policy," but also decries the failure to put global justice issues, particularly global poverty, at the centre of the agenda.[13] Project Ploughshares, which is the churches' ecumenical peace centre, suggests that five "Ds" would be more appropriate, adding democracy and disarmament to the list. The KAIROS coalition of Canadian churches has called for a rights-based framework to underpin Canadian foreign policy, an approach that would focus on the causes of global insecurity, such as the growing disparity between rich and poor, regional conflict, economic domination, and ecological degradation. The churches continue to advocate for peace-building, economic and ecological justice, and human rights as cornerstones of Canada's foreign policy. Unfortunately, the IPS reflects the government's overarching commitment to a neo-liberal, free trade economic model that excludes and oppresses the poor majority. The goals of global justice, promoting Canada's international human rights obligations, and the eradication of poverty are relegated to the margins of the IPS.

Returning to the matter of Haiti, there are a total of twenty-four references to the nation in four of the five sections of the IPS; the country does not appear in the commerce section. Almost every reference to Haiti links it to a short list of countries (often Afghanistan and Somalia) which are considered "failed and fragile states." I do not question the policy focus on failed and fragile states, but I do agree with the CCIC that the IPS "puts undue emphasis on perceived threats to Canada's security emanating from failed and fragile states."[14] In reality, the usual victims in failed states are the citizens of those states.[15] As the CCIC points out, the government should focus on social and economic reconstruction, conflict management, and peace-building in failed and fragile states, drawing on the expertise of people with long histories of work in specific contexts.

Furthermore, the IPS overlooks Canada's own role in fomenting instability. Canada regularly repatriates foreign-born criminals who have not obtained citizenship prior to their convictions. Moreover, its immigration policies siphon away the skilled and educated from Haiti and other developing countries. Indeed, the World Bank recently pointed out that eight out of every ten Haitians and Jamaicans with university degrees live outside the country of their birth.[16] Finally, the trade liberalization policies promoted by Canada and others have caused great damage to Haitian agriculture and rural communities, particularly peasant producers. Non-state actors, including local change agents, are either ignored in the IPS, or treated simply as implementers of government policy. The notion of addressing poverty as a fundamental human rights obligation is absent.

Haiti requires a more sophisticated approach than that advocated in the IPS. An emphasis on failed states that emphasizes security over poverty will not address Haiti's problems. Moreover, the specific references to Haiti in the IPS betray an orientation toward fixing the "state" as the solution to problems of poverty or security or the failure to respect human rights. There is a wide body of literature about the distinction in Haiti between "state" and "nation." Anthropogist Michel-Rolph Trouillot argues in his illuminating account of

Duvalierism, *Haiti: State Against Nation,* that the Haitian state is relatively autonomous from the nation: all problems are turned into political problems, but a distinction needs to be made between the state, much less the political class, and society. If foreign donors listen, they may find that the Haitian people have a project that is different from that imagined in the proposed solutions that focus too narrowly on the state.[17s] Haiti scholar Robert Maguire (see chapter 2) recently told the Washington Post that "Haiti has suffered years of mis-governance, with its leaders too often putting their interests ahead of those of the country and its citizens. As a result the Haitian 'state' has never really invested in the Haitian 'nation.'"[18]

Fixing the Haitian state in its various manifestations may be a worthwhile goal, if only in the short term to mitigate its more predatory aspects. But making the state work better is not sufficient. Over the longer term, the state must function to ensure the protection of human rights and to create greater social justice for all Haitians. The interim government has largely failed to advance this agenda. Although attention is paid to rebuilding the Haitian state, it is at least as important to attend to the needs of the Haitian people. Haitian churches and NGOs and their international partners are uniquely positioned to assist with these tasks. Solid investment in the Haitian people, particularly in education, support for the rural sector, urban renewal, and secure livelihoods, will produce better results over the long term than state-centred security efforts.[19] HIV/AIDS is still a huge challenge in Haiti, but so are other health issues. More attention needs to be paid to environmental protection and to disaster prevention. Training of police forces needs to be matched with judicial and penal reform.

A concerted effort must be made by the international community to avoid the kind of fatigue that can set in when donors realize that development which produces positive change for all Haitians takes many years to come about. Recent experience shows that aid from abroad declined steadily in the years after the end of military rule in 1994, falling from a high of US$611 million in 1995 to a low of US$136 million in 2002.[20]

Meanwhile, foreign NGOs and churches like the United Church of Canada will continue to support the work of their partners who seek to empower the majority of Haitians through grassroots organizations and networks, where hope persists against all odds. They will continue to join in solidarity with those who criticize emerging mechanisms that further marginalize the Haitian people, and support those who seek social and economic alternatives that promote democratic and progressive development. Those who seek to be in solidarity with Haiti need to listen more attentively to the diverse sub-groups within the Haitian nation.[21] Over time, Haitians themselves will create the channels through which all sectors can participate in society.

Notes

1   L'Institut Culturel Karl Lévêque (ICKL) <www.ickl-haiti.org> is a private, non-confessional, non-profit foundation, and it is not tied to any political party. Created in July 1989, ICKL defines itself as a centre for reflection, social analysis, and popular education. It sees itself extending its contribution to the struggles for liberation of the popular sectors of society through reflection on theory, analysis, and accompaniment of grassroots groups. ICKL participates in the Haitian Advocacy Platform for Alternative Development (PAPDA). See <http://www.rehred-haiti.net/membres/papda/INTROPAPDA.htm>. Accessed October 2005.

2   The best-known leader of the G-184 was also the country's largest employer: Andy Apaid, Jr., a factory owner born in the United States. See Human Rights Watch, <http://hrw.org/english/docs/2004/02/27/haiti7677.htm>. Accessed October 2005.

3   Thomas Jefferson, for example, argued that the "contagion" of black liberty had to be confined to the island.

4   Center for Cooperative Research, "US-Haiti timeline." Available at: <http://www.cooperativeresearch.org/timeline.jsp?timeline=haiti>. Accessed October 2005.

5   CNN, "Clinton urges Aristide to resolve Haiti's electoral impasse," 7 December 2000. <http://archives.cnn.com/2000/WORLD/americas/12/07/haiti.clinton.ap/>. Accessed October 2005.

6   Mary Turck, Resource Center of the Americas, "Haiti Q and A," 23 February 2004. Available at: <http://www.americas.org/index.php?cp=item&item_id=13759>. Accessed October 2005.

7   Anthony Fenton, The Dominion Daily Weblog, 15 September 2004. Available at: <http://dominionpaper.ca/weblog/2004/09/interview_with_denis_paradis_on_haiti_regime_change.html>. Accessed October 2005.

8   François L'Écuyer, «Haïti: Le débat qui divise la gauche,» *Alternatives,* 17 octobre 2005. Available at: <http://www.alternatives.ca/article2117.html>. Accessed October 2005.

9   See, for example, Kevin Skerritt, "Faking Genocide in Haiti: Canada's Role in the Persecution of Yvon Neptune." Available at: <http://www.zmag.org/content/showarticle.cfm?SectionID=55&ItemID=8144>. Accessed October 2005.

10   See <http://www.united-church.ca/justice/news/haiti/040316.shtm>. Accessed October 2005.

11   "Initial Considerations of the International Mission," 8 April 2005. Available at: <http://www.jubileesouth.org/sp/index.php?category=5&id=154>. Accessed October 2005.

12   «Il s'agit maintenant d'aider les secteurs populaires à se restructurer afin de mettre en place cette force alternative en vue de parvenir à une autonomie et une indépendance réelles.» Marc Arthur Fils-Aimé, Institut Culturel Karl Lévêque, IIIe Sommet des Peuples, Mar del Plata, Alterpresse, 3 November 2005. Available at: <http://www.alterpresse.org/article.php3?id_article=3508>. Accessed October 2005.

13   Canadian Council for International Cooperation, "Commentary on Canada's International Policy Statement," 30 April 2005, p. 1. Available at: <http://www.ccic.ca/e/

home/index.shtml>. Accessed October 2005. For the KAIROS brief, see <http://www
.kairoscanada.org/e/index.asp>. Accessed October 2005. For the Project Ploughshares
brief, see <http://www.ploughshares.ca/>. Accessed October 2005.

14 CCIC, "Commentary," 5.

15 On a related note, the word "security" appears eighty-eight times in the Overview
section of the IPS, only three times as "human security," and the word "poverty"
appears only twelve times.

16 "Where brain drains lead," *The Globe and Mail*, 31 October 2005, A12.

17 Michel-Rolph Trouillot, *Haiti: State against Nation: The Origins and Legacy of Duvalierism* (New York: Monthly Review Press, 1990).

18 Robert Maguire, Director of International Affairs and Haiti Programs, Trinity College,
"Transcript: Haiti Crisis," 1 March 2004. Available at: <http://www.washington
post.com/wp-dyn/articles/A13187–2004Feb27.html>. Accessed October 2005.

19 For a good example of recent NGO views on development priorities in Haiti, see
« Position de la Coordination Europe-Haïti en vue de la Conférence Ministérielle
pour Haïti » : Bruxelles, le 20 et 21 octobre 2005. Available at: <http://www.rehred-
haiti.net/membres/papda/CoEHoct05.htm>. Accessed October 2005.

20 *The New York Times*, 14 July 2004. <http://www.nytimes.com/2004/07/14/politics/
14hait.html>. Accessed October 2005.

21 Trouillot, *Haiti: State against Nation,* 230.

Conclusion

La difficile sortie d'une longue transition

SUZY CASTOR

Dans le cadre d'un processus complexe de transition à la démocratie, Haïti vit une profonde crise institutionnelle qui, dans ses expressions pluri-dimensionnelles, se situe dans une trajectoire d'épuisement et de difficile renouvellement du système socio-économique et politique. Elle charrie les conséquences de la longue dictature des Duvalier et aussi les vicissitudes des deux décennies de luttes sociales et politiques. Ces facteurs, avec comme toile de fond l'accentuation de la détérioration socio-économique, ont dégradé le tissu démocratique, brisé l'élan participatif de la population et contribué à déstructurer l'économie et la société en général.

La Toile de Fond

D'entrée de jeu, je ferai ici trois considérations : l'ampleur de la pauvreté et de l'exclusion, la nature politique de la conjoncture actuelle et le caractère de la longue transition ouverte en 1986.

La pauvreté et l'exclusion *L'ampleur de la pauvreté et de l'exclusion* est intolérable. Même si l'apparente froideur des indices de services de base ne révèle pas pleinement la réalité violente que vit au quotidien une grande partie de la population haïtienne, ces chiffres ne permettent à personne d'escamoter l'ampleur du phénomène de la pauvreté. Ils ont comme corollaire le phé-

---

A version of this chapter was delivered as an address on October 4, 2005, and was updated following the presidential elections of February 7, 2006.

nomène de l'exclusion qui tend à s'accroître, affectant de plus en plus des milliers d'Haïtiens et d'Haïtiennes qui affrontent au quotidien l'absence des éléments essentiels qui permettent à tout individu de vivre et de s'épanouir moralement et physiquement au sein d'une société (50 % de la population n'a pas accès à l'eau potable; 80 % de la population rurale vit au-dessous du niveau de pauvreté absolue). Cette situation insère en elle-même une violence qui peut être explosive. Des situations semblables se retrouvent dans bon nombre des pays du Tiers Monde, mais il y a une grande différence : tandis que partout ailleurs il existe des poches plus ou moins étendues de pauvreté, en Haïti elle affecte le plus grand pourcentage de la population où près des deux tiers vivent au dessous du seuil de pauvreté. Cette situation est d'autant plus inquiétante que depuis des décennies on peut parler d'un développement bloqué.

La nature politique de la conjoncture *La conjoncture actuelle est éminemment politique, et la résolution de la question de la direction politique acquiert un poids insoupçonné.* L'archaïsme du système politique et l'incapacité de l'Etat à remplir ses fonctions projette de façon évidente la nécessité de la modernisation de l'Etat et du système politique. Cela se doit non seulement à cause du rôle qu'a toujours joué l'Etat dans la structuration de notre société mais aussi parce que la sortie de cette crise passe par le renforcement des structures d'Etat et de l'institutionnalisation, le fonctionnement des partis politiques, l'organisation de la société civile, l'existence d'une citoyenneté pour tous et la volonté politique nécessaire pour entreprendre les réformes indispensables pour la construction de la nation.

Les problèmes de santé, d'éducation, d'infrastructures, de logements, de lutte contre la pauvreté, etc. ne peuvent être considérés seulement sous les aspects techniques ou sociaux en dehors du politique. Seul un leadership constitué et organisé sera capable de donner confiance à la population et de propulser les valeurs d'efficacité, de solidarité humaine et d'intérêts collectifs, ainsi qu'un projet national indispensable pour la cohérence même de n'importe quelle action dans ces domaines.

Le caractère de la longue transition *La transition ouverte en 1986, dominée en grande partie par le régime Lavalas, évolua d'un grand enthousiasme vers le désenchantement.* De façon évidente elle n'a pas atteint les objectifs indispensables recherchés dès le début : l'institutionnalisation démocratique, la consolidation de l'Etat de droit, la diminution des inégalités socio-économiques et le démarrage économique. De là, la polarisation de certaines des contradictions et confrontations qui secouent cette société de carence.

Pour comprendre cette longue transition, bien que le projecteur de l'histoire se révèle indispensable pour éclairer l'itinéraire de cette nation qui lutte pour se construire de façon légitime et pour satisfaire ses nécessités de développement et de modernisation, je n'en signalerai que quelques caractéristiques, dans une tentative de comprendre et de ne pas perdre l'essentiel du processus.

La multiplicité des acteurs qui rentrent sur la scène, ou pour le moins qui acquièrent une certaine visibilité, « complique » la vie politique traditionnelle. Les exclus de toujours, la paysannerie, qui depuis l'occupation nord-américaine du commencement du siècle (1915–1934) avait été refoulée, resurgit dans le plan revendicatif et citoyen. La population des nouveaux bidonvilles surgis au cours des dernières années, les classes moyennes et les habitants des provinces s'affrontent aux acteurs traditionnels affaiblis. L'Eglise catholique et les secteurs de la bourgeoisie n'arrivent pas à visualiser les mutations qui s'opèrent au sein de la société. Enfin if faut signaler le rôle omniprésent de la communauté internationale qui acquiert un poids surdéterminant dans les prises de décision.

Cette longue et difficile transition avec les racines historiques d'une profonde crise exprime les turbulences d'une société segmentée et atomisée avec des mutations au niveau de l'Etat, de l'économie et de la culture qui lui fait perdre sa cohérence séculaire. Contestée par les élites traditionnelles, par les puissances internationales et par les nouveaux acteurs, le régime politique perd donc sa propre légitimité.

Dans ce contexte de contestation constante et presque unanime, *les méthodes de contention, de cooptation, de domination et de répression traditionnelle perdent de leur efficacité.* Face aux demandes de ces nouveaux acteurs collectifs, le régime politique affaibli met à nu son incapacité de gouverner, de répondre aux exigences de participation, d'assurer le développement du pays et le bien-être de la population et de maintenir la cohésion sociale.

Il faut rappeler ici le caractère irréconciliable et très tendu de cette lutte qui a toujours été pacifique et marquée par la primauté du politique. Les militaires au pouvoir, et plus tard Jean-Bertrand Aristide, voulurent dévier celle-ci en utilisant la grande masse dépourvue mais disponible et cherchèrent à l'orienter vers un certain niveau de violence. Dans une tentative perverse, le pouvoir arma une partie de la population, particulièrement celle des bidonvilles de la zone métropolitaine. Pour cela aujourd'hui la vision violente que projette la lutte haïtienne doit se mesurer à sa juste valeur, quand on pense que durant ces dernières années seulement 3 000 policiers assuraient le maintien de l'ordre pour plus de 8 millions d'habitants. Cependant, il nous faut faire le douloureux constat que toute la violence inhérente à cette longue transition a laissé Haïti divisée et détruite comme si elle avait été un pays en guerre, et l'a convertie virtuellement en l'une des zones les plus explosives du continent.

La construction de l'Etat-nation aujourd'hui pose un défi gigantesque. Il faut réaliser *en même temps* la modernisation institutionnelle de l'Etat et du système politique, le développement économique et la justice sociale ou la citoyenneté pour tous, dans un contexte de présence étrangère, quelle que soit sa signification. A cause de son caractère historico structurel et son degré de maturité, la crise actuelle se nie à toute tentative de recomposition. En même temps, malgré les luttes sociales rénovées avec leurs avances notoires et leurs échecs évidents, la société n'arrive pas encore à se doter d'une nouvelle structure capable de lui permettre de sortir de la crise et de provoquer le "take-off." Aucun secteur social ou politique n'arrive encore à résoudre le problème de la direction politique et économique du pays. La question de l'hégémonie posée depuis la fin du XIXe siècle n'arrive pas à se résoudre car, d'une part, la vieille oligarchie épuisée n'arrive pas à rénover le système socio-économique et politique et, d'autre part, le mouvement social, puissant en son essence mais faible dans son organisation et dans ses manifestations, souffre du manque de ressources et surtout de l'absence du moteur de partis politiques forts. Ces derniers, à leur tour, souffrent de l'absence de dynamisme des organisations structurées de la société civile.

Pour cela le thème de la refondation nationale s'est transformé en un des concepts clés de cette période. Malgré les interprétations ou positions très diverses sur les causes et la nature des problèmes ainsi que sur les alternatives pour résoudre la problématique de l'anachronisme social, économique et politique dans une rénovation nécessaire et urgente des bases de la nation, un accord tacite semble régner au sein de tous les secteurs sociaux.

Les Défis Immediats

La réalisation des élections   La campagne en vue des élections a tous les niveaux – municipales, parlementaires et présidentielles – commença officiellement le 8 octobre 2005. S'ouvrit donc une nouvelle étape difficile, pleine de dangers avec les vieux démons d'hier et d'aujourd'hui. Les élections constituent un passage obligé pour sortir de la crise. Elles peuvent être considérées comme un acte fondateur, car elles doivent assurer la légitimité du nouveau gouvernement, permettre de mettre en marche les institutions essentielles de l'Etat et clarifier l'échiquier politique par une décantation des forces politiques. Sans être une panacée, et loin de là, ces élections doivent constituer le point de départ d'un long et laborieux processus d'institutionnalisation de la démocratie et de l'instauration d'un régime de droit.

Cependant, de grandes appréhensions et inquiétudes, voire un certain scepticisme, hantaient l'esprit de larges secteurs aussi bien nationaux qu'internationaux quant à leur réalisation. Les réitérations officielles proclamaient haut et fort, avec plus ou moins de conviction, que les élections se réaliseraient de façon inéluctable et que le prochain gouvernement prendrait possession du pouvoir le 7 février, « date inamovible », malgré les obstacles qui cependant restaient multiples.

Tout d'abord le Conseil électoral provisoire (CEP), institution constitutionnelle qui a en charge la réalisation des élections, a montré de tels atermoiements et faiblesses dans son aspect organisationnel et de gestion, a connu dans son sein de si multiples luttes pour le pouvoir, a provoqué de tels conflits et accumulé de tels retards et ratés dans l'organisation des opérations pré-électorales (inscription des électeurs et électrices, particulièrement dans le milieu rural, distribution des bureaux d'inscription, disponibilité des cartes électorales, etc.), a démontré une absence de maîtrise du processus (report en 4 fois de la date officielle des élections, incapacité jusqu'au derniers moments de publier les listes des candidats admis a participer aux joutes électorales) que beaucoup, dans le meilleur des cas, doutaient de sa volonté sinon de sa capacité de respecter les échéances électorales.

Pour faire face à cette situation, certains secteurs – et non des moindres – prônaient le remplacement pur et simple du CEP, considérant comme peine perdue tout rafistolage possible. Cependant, sous la pression de l'opinion publique, des partis politiques, de la communauté internationale et à la recherche d'une certaine efficacité – et malgré les dangers d'une mise en place d'une superstructure non prévue constitutionnellement, et à peine à deux mois de la tenue des comices – le gouvernement choisit plutôt de renforcer le CEP par la nomination d'un comite d'appui et d'un directeur exécutif afin de dynamiser l'organisme électoral et de « remettre le processus électoral sur les rails ».

Vu leur importance, ces élections se devaient d'offrir toutes les garanties de sérieux dans leur déroulement et favoriser la plus grande participation populaire. Il a été évident durant tout le processus électoral que cet aspect, en particulier, représentait un enjeu majeur, car, si la participation était faible elle risquait de fragiliser et d'affecter la légitimité du nouveau pouvoir et d'ouvrir la voie à une nouvelle période d'instabilité politique. Malgré des erreurs évidentes et des lenteurs impardonnables, l'inscription des électeurs atteint cependant, un niveau acceptable : des 4 millions d'électeurs potentiels, plus de 3,2 millions inscrits, soit plus de 70 % de l'électorat. Il était clair que la population en général, pour des raisons diverses, voulait exercer son droit citoyen.

Jamais aucun processus électoral en Haïti n'a connu une surveillance internationale et nationale tellement haute, d'autant plus que les difficultés de nature diverse se multipliaient.

Il faut d'abord signaler les difficultés purement techniques ou administratives : la complexité des bulletins électoraux, pour une population majoritairement analphabète; le recours, en dernière instance, à la Cour de cassation introduit par la dernière loi électorale, le surgissement d'imbroglio politico judiciaire non prévu, les interprétations sur la nationalité des candidats, l'ajournement de la date des élections, le non respect du calendrier constitutionnel, la non localisation des centres et des bureaux de vote etc.; avec les complications techniques inhérentes à la réalisation de toutes élections, depuis la distribution des kits électoraux jusqu'au déploiement du personnel sur le terrain.

Vinrent aussi celles de caractère politique. Certains secteurs ne voulaient pas de leur réalisation. De bonne foi, quelques-uns avançaient qu'il fallait d'abord s'attaquer aux problèmes cruciaux avant leur réalisation. D'autres pensaient qu'aucune élection n'était possible avec la présence des troupes étrangères, et que par conséquent celles-ci ne représenteraient qu'une tape à l'œil. D'autre part, Jean-Bertrand Aristide, qui rêve d'un retour en Haïti et du contrôle du pouvoir, luttait par tous les moyens pour dominer la scène politique et comme toujours conservait deux fers au feu : veut pas mais veut au cas ou aucune manœuvre ne pouvait les empêcher. De même, d'autres secteurs politiques et économiques ne se sentant pas encore prêts pour affronter ces joutes, ou jouissant de la situation troublée actuelle pour consolider des négoces illicites, ne voulaient pas considérer la perspective d'un changement.

Enfin un élément, et non des moindres : les difficultés financières. Le coût de l'organisation des élections est estimé à 60 millions de dollars, dont 90 % sont fournis par la communauté internationale. Le déficit de 4,1 millions de dollars enregistré dans leur financement semble avoir trouver une solution lors de la dernière réunion de Bruxelles. Ici, il faut souligner la nécessité de promouvoir de sérieuses réflexions sur la tenue des élections dans le monde d'aujourd'hui. D'une part les modalités techniques de réalisation et le coût des comices pour l'accomplissement de cet acte citoyen indispensable à la vie sociétale, atteignent un niveau de sophistication accrue. Par conséquent, les dépenses exigées ne peuvent pas être supportés par les pays pauvres comme

Haïti, ce qui, en définitive, augmentent de façon notoire une dépendance accrue de la communauté internationale.

Le système électoral haïtien rentre à n'en pas douter dans une étape de modernisation caractérisée par l'utilisation d'une nouvelle technologie dans les centres électoraux, par la réalisation de sondages répétés, par l'utilisation de communication moderne etc. Mais aussi, à la fois jamais le poids de l'international n'a été aussi lourd ni aussi au delà de l'appui technique.

La problématique de la sécurité a constitué l'un des facteurs qui devrait contribuer en grande mesure, à asseoir la qualité, la participation et la réussite ou pas des joutes électorales. Tout en reconnaissant les efforts déployés sur ce plan et les progrès relatifs mais indéniables réalisés, diverses instances ont exhorté le chef du gouvernement intérimaire à garantir la tenue opportune et dans de bonnes conditions des élections générales qui doivent boucler la période provisoire. A tour de rôle ont exprimé leurs préoccupations sur cette question le Secrétaire Général et le Conseil de Sécurité des Nations Unies, le Congrès nord-américain et le gouvernement français. Ce point, dans l'actuelle conjoncture représentait un vrai défi, face aux revendications de sécurité de la population pour leur vécu au quotidien et pour la bonne réalisation des élections.

La sécurité La question de la sécurité devient l'un des items les plus marquants de la conjoncture. Nous ne nous référons pas au problème chronique de petit banditisme dû en grande partie à la situation de misère et de détérioration du pays, mais à une situation déclenchée particulièrement depuis septembre 2004, avec *l'opération Bagdad*. Fondamentalement circonscrite à Port-au-Prince, cette violence tend cependant à s'étendre dans les provinces et à atteindre des niveaux alarmants.

Les acteurs sont divers. Ce sont d'abord les « chimères » se réclamant de Jean-Bertrand Aristide, qui ont évolué vers une structure qui semble autonome et qui occupent les principaux bidonvilles et certains quartiers de la zone métropolitaine, les transformant en zone de non loi. Il faut y ajouter d'autres acteurs avec des mobiles diffus qui se retrouvent dans un entrecroisement à la fois politique, économique et maffieux. Ici doit être mentionnée de façon spéciale l'influence des délinquants reconnus coupables et condamnés par la justice américaine, et aussi bien qu'en moindre mesure, canadienne qui sont systématiquement refoulés et déportés sans autre forme de procès en Haïti, leur pays d'origine. Inutile de souligner l'absence d'infrastructure d'accueil et de suivi de ces criminels très souvent dangereux et sophistiqués dans leurs méthodes d'opérer. Incrustés essentiellement à Port-au-Prince, et dans une bien moindre mesure dans deux ou trois villes de province, ils maintiennent en alerte de façon constante la population et particulièrement ont recours au kidnapping. Ce phénomène jusque là inconnu en Haïti, se circonscrivait, à ses débuts, aux riches personnalités du secteur des affaires à ses débuts, mais aujourd'hui il a pris beaucoup plus d'ampleur et s'étend à toute la population. Le constat d'impuissance et de désespoir qui accable de larges couches de la société haïtienne crée un cercle vicieux, augmente le sentiment d'insécurité et enhardit d'avantage les bandits, ce qui s'est traduit par une vraie psychose au cours du premier semestre 2005, fermant un cercle vicieux : violence, insécurité, impunité.

Il faut rappeler ici que l'approche erronée de la question de l'insécurité par la Mission des Nations Unies pour la stabilisation en Haïti (MINUSTAH), lui attribuant primordialement, sinon exclusivement, une cause sociale et sous-estimant sa caractéristique politique, contribua à rénforcer l'organisation de ce mercenariat d'un nouveau type et dans une certaine mesure la consolidation de ces gangs. Après la culmination à un niveau intolérable de l'insécurité à partir des mois mai-juin 2005 et l'assassinat du jeune poète kidnappé, Jacques Roche, la lutte pour le démantèlement des gangs entra dans une nouvelle étape. Mais elle se révèle d'autant plus difficile que ceux-ci avaient eu le temps de se consolider. Cette approche aurait conduit la MINUSTAH à privilégier presque exclusivement un seul instrument de combat et expliquerait, en partie, le fait qu'elle n'ait pas mis sur pied, dès le début, un service efficace de renseignement.

La question de la sécurité, qui doit être attaquée par des moyens divers, est indissociablement liée à celle du désarmement général. Selon certaines estimations, le régime Lavalas avait, à la fin de son règne, distribué à ses partisans quelque vingt mille armes, qui se sont ajoutés à ceux déjà existants dans les secteurs de Lavalas et des groupes interlopes. Parallèlement, les anciens militaires du mouvement armé de fin 2003–2004, revendiquant la restauration de l'armée d'Haïti, n'ont jamais mis bas les armes. Des rumeurs persistantes signalent l'arrivée continue, dès le 29 février 2004, d'armes destinées à tous ces secteurs. Cette situation qui existait dès les premiers mois de l'administration Alexandre-Latortue constitue aujourd'hui encore, de l'avis de plus d'un, l'un des plus graves problèmes de la conjoncture.

Immédiatement se pose donc la question de la Police nationale d'Haïti (PNH). Ce n'est pas le lieu ici de faire l'historique de cette police surgie après la dissolution de l'armée par Jean-Bertrand Aristide en 1995, qui porte dans son évolution les vicissitudes et les tares de sa genèse. Cette institution joue un rôle capital dans la considération de l'évolution du pays et du processus électoral et post-électoral. Il faut rappeler que la formation d'une police professionnelle au service de la population a été une occasion manquée en 1995. La création de la police connut une grande popularité et un appui extraordinaire entre les jeunes et la population en générale, qui avaient rejeté l'armée honnie à cause de ses exactions. Cependant, elle fut vite pervertie à la fois par la surpolitisation menée par Jean-Bertrand Aristide et la lutte maffieuse qui se livra pour son contrôle. Le recrutement dès lors favorisa l'établissement des sphères d'influence et en consolida d'autres provenant des structures de l'ancienne armée ou des nouveaux venus au pouvoir.

Au lendemain du 29 février 2004, on pouvait parler d'un effondrement de cette institution suite à la politisation systématique, la corruption et la désinstitutionalisation. L'une des priorités d'alors était le redressement de la PNH. L'opacité avec laquelle le gouvernement intérimaire aborda alors la réforme n'a pas fait avancer la restructuration ni l'épuration au sein de la police tel que le pays – et d'ailleurs l'institution elle-même – s'y attendait. Une bonne reforme aurait été à n'en pas douter plus facile à réaliser à ce moment.

Aujourd'hui, le redressement de la PNH, malgré la présence de policiers honnêtes, capables et animés d'un bon esprit de corps, doit s'affronter à des difficultés que je citerai ici pêle-mêle : les antagonismes policiers-militaires; les relents du comportement de l'ancienne armée; les violations des droits de l'homme dans les commissariats; l'existence de cadres corrompus et criminels; la rupture des chaînes de commandement selon l'avis même de l'actuel directeur de la police, Mario Andresol; le dysfonctionnement de la justice haïtienne, qui favorise l'impunité; le problème des militaires démobilisés; la carence de ressources matérielles, d'infrastructures physiques, d'armements et de moyens financiers; l'utilisation irrationnelle des ressources disponibles; la nécessité d'une vraie dépuration.

Les derniers remaniements au sein de cette institution permettront-ils d'affronter ces problèmes, ou tout au moins permettront-ils au prochain gouvernement d'avoir les bases adéquates pour arriver à une vraie restructuration et répondre à l'urgent redressement de la PNH. Il faudra attendre avant de pouvoir répondre à cette question.

Face à cette réalité, revient de façon lancinante la question de la reconstitution de l'armée. Elle s'impose d'autant plus que le développement de l'insécurité provoque, semble-t-il, une amnésie en relation au comportement des anciennes Forces armées d'Haïti et les projete comme seules capables d'assurer l'ordre. Cette question est d'autant plus délicate qu'elle gagne du terrain de plus en plus. On a vite oublié que selon les témoignages de ses propres intégrants, l'armée d'Haïti, fille de la gendarmerie haïtienne créée par l'occupation américaine, remplissait 10 % de fonctions militaires et 85 % de fonctions policières. Il est nécessaire de développer au sein de la PNH des unités spécialisées pour la lutte contre le grand banditisme, la garde frontalière, etc. Cependant, la reconstitution de l'armée, outre ces implications politiques et de droits humains, représenterait un retour vers le passé et une charge économique si lourde qu'elle répercuterait sur tout projet national de développement. D'où l'urgente nécessité d'un accord national sur ce thème. Toutefois, s'impose de façon primordiale une nouvelle structuration, dépuration et professionnalisation de la police en évitant les erreurs d'un passé encore récent afin d'assurer la sécurité publique.

Les Acteurs

Le gouvernement Dès son installation, il était clair que le gouvernement intérimaire, qui ne disposait pas d'une assise politique populaire, avait une double mission. D'une part, il devait mettre en marche et faire fonctionner l'appareil d'Etat complètement détruit; réaliser les réformes indispensables pour renforcer l'institutionnalité; combattre l'insécurité de façon à ce que le prochain gouvernement, avec toute la légitimité que lui conféreraient les élections, trouve un chemin aplani pour enfin mettre le pays sur les rails de la modernité, du droit et de la justice sociale. Et, d'autre part, il devait aussi contribuer à créer les conditions nécessaires pour réaliser de bonnes élections et assurer la passation de pouvoir après les scrutins.

On peut signaler à l'actif du gouvernement intérimaire la non-utilisation de la répression comme arme politique pour combattre des adversaires et aussi le non-recours à l'insécurité comme moyen de se maintenir au pouvoir. Cependant, ses hésitations, ses indéfinitions, ses confusions entre la chasse aux sorcières et l'impunité et son laxisme sur des questions primordiales ont contribué à faire pourrir la situation et à la compliquer. Dix-huit mois après son installation, le gouvernement Boniface-Latortue se retrouvait bien loin des réalisations attendues.

Quant aux élections, après une valse lente incompréhensible, les autorités gouvernementales ont manifesté a maintes reprises une accélération intruse qui risquait à certains moments de télescoper l'action du Conseil Electoral Provisoire, dans leur initiative pour accélérer le processus électoral et le sortir de l'impasse qui semblait se dessiner.

Les partis politiques Il n'est un secret pour aucun de ceux qui connaissent la situation haïtienne que l'existence et le fonctionnement de partis politiques sont encore récents en Haïti. On peut situer vers 1986 l'entrée des partis politiques sur la scène avec toutes les déformations, perversions et difficultés d'une implantation réalisée dans un climat d'hostilité généralisée face aux partis.

Aujourd'hui on peut dire que l'on a beaucoup avancé. Les diverses lois électorales favorisent la formation de partis et de coalitions de partis. Bien que fortement critiqué ou rejeté par une grande partie de l'opinion publique, paradoxalement le rôle des partis commence à être compris et jugé indispensable dans le fonctionnement de toute société démocratique. Naturellement, la pléthore de ceux qui venaient aux courses récentes électorales (quarante-trois partis) est devenue presque caricaturale. Cependant, il ne faut pas tellement s'alarmer ou jeter la première pierre, parce que cette réalité s'enregistre dans les pays où les époques de dictature longue ou d'absence d'institutionnalisation se sont soldées par des situations identiques. En réalité, il est connu de tous que seulement six ou sept partis au plus constituent des partenaires réels dans cette course électorale.

D'une part il y a le courant Lavalas dans une dispute, momentanée, peut être même, en grande partie, apparente pour assurer la réorganisation d'un nouveau leadership du mouvement, parce que malgré une présence actuelle sur la scène politique et le déploiement de diverses manœuvres, le leadership de Jean-Bertrand Aristide a beaucoup diminué et tendra à s'effriter. La figure de René Préval domine le panorama Lavalas, et ce ne serait pas étonnant de voir se ranger autour de lui plusieurs factions Lavalas, qui aujourd'hui sembleraient encore antagoniques.

Des secteurs politiques et sociaux importants appréhendent d'une part la répétition et les conséquences de l'expérience de la présidence de doublure de Préval I. D'autre part les conséquences perverses de l'anarchisme et du populisme de ces mêmes acteurs qui ont dominé pendant plus de 13 ans la scène politique et qui revenaient au niveau de la campagne électorale.

D'autre part, il y a le grand éventail de partis du centre gauche au centre droit qui ont déjà l'âge de raison (au moins sept ans d'existence) et qui possède une quelconque structure et organisation. Face aux enjeux de la lutte électorale, ils réalisent des regroupements, quelquefois contre nature, mais bien que fragmentés ils restent tous conscients qu'en ordre dispersé ils diminuent aussi leur chance de parvenir au pouvoir. Bien que certains prônent dès maintenant une alliance ou une fusion, il existe peu de possibilités pour que celle-ci arrive à se concrétiser dès le premier tour.

Enfin, comme troisième catégorie, il faut souligner la présence de partis politiques surgis comme des champignons au cours de ces dernières années et même de ces derniers mois, qui n'ont de parti que le nom. Font partie également de cette catégorie, des individus et personnalités provenant de la société civile qui espèrent suppléer à leur manque de structure organisationnel par l'utilisation de grands moyens économiques. Très souvent, nombre d'entre eux se lancent dans la campagne électorale à la recherche du prestige d'avoir été candidat à la présidence ou de la protection d'une certaine immunité parlementaire.

Malgré la réclamation de plus en plus courante au sein de l'électorat de la présentation de programmes, dans ces élections la personnalité du (ou de la) candidat(e) est l'élément clef qui guide le choix de la population à la recherche d'un homme ou d'une femme, au passé propre, honnête, énergique, capable d'entreprendre le chemin de la reconstruction tant rêvé. Avec une telle situation il sera très difficile aux candidats de quelque soit la formation politique de réussir au premier tour. A la fois, on peut envisager déja un grand éparpillement de tendances au sein du Grand Corps.

Un fait est certain : si les partis de plus d'enracinement dans le milieu souffrent d'un manque de savoir faire et de tradition, ce qui leur fera d'avantage défaut dans ces joutes c'est le manque de moyens financiers. Le financement des partis politiques prévu par la loi électorale, étant une donne très délicate, n'a pas pu se concrétiser jusqu'à présent que çe soit au niveau du gouvernement, de la loi électorale ou de la communauté internationale. Cette question revient toujours sur le tapis, mais sans solution comme l'attestent les déclarations du gouvernement haïtien ou les conclusions de plusieurs réunions internationales, dont la toute dernière à Bruxelles ou le IVe sommet des Amériques qui se tenait en Argentine.

Cependant, ces atermoiements semblent ignorer un danger réel. Ceux qui disposent de plus grands moyens financiers – provenant directement ou indirectement à des sources liées aux activités illicites – pourraient gagner par les urnes les postes électifs et occuper les avenues des structures d'Etat. Cette réalité nous invite à toute une réflexion dans ce domaine.

Méritent d'être encouragées certaines éclaircies dans les pratiques politiques : d'une part malgré ses limitations, sincérité ou application, un code de conduite électorale a été signé entre divers partis, de même que le pacte de stabilité et de gouvernabilité qui prévoit la période post-électorale, avec le fonctionnement d'une opposition et l'application d'un plan de gouvernement.

La Société Civile Comme les partis politiques, la société civile haïtienne est encore atomisée et manque de la cohésion nécessaire pour bien jouer son rôle à la fois multiforme et indispensable dans la transition. Malgré les difficultés inhérentes à l'avance globale de la société en générale, la réorganisation et le renforcement des organisations de la société civile semblent avancer. Son poids est d'une importance capitale dans la mobilisation en faveur des élections et dans sa participation à la grande tâche de reconstruction nationale.

La communauté internationale La résolution 1529 de février 2004 sur Haïti adoptée par le Conseil de sécurité des Nations Unies accorde, pour stabiliser le pays, le déploiement immédiat d'une force rapide intérimaire suivie d'une mission de maintien de la paix (MINUSTAH) avec l'établissement d'une force multinationale pour assurer une intervention à long terme par les Nations Unies.

Il n'y a pas de doute que la présence de cette mission de stabilisation ait un contenu différent des traditionnelles interventions militaires dans le continent et en Haïti durant le XXe siècle. Cette force de paix, au moment de son entrée en scène, avait exercé un pouvoir de contention qui a empêché tout au moins le chaos programmé par le régime anarcho-populiste en déroute de Jean-Bertrand Aristide. Maintenant, en dépit de certains échos provenant de sources intéressées avec des objectifs inavouables faisant état d'une prochaine vraie occupation, selon les règles d'un protectorat ou réclamant la mise sous tutelle d'Haïti vu l'incapacité des Haïtiens et Haïtiennes, cette force doit conserver son caractère et ne pas dévier de sa mission ou tomber dans la tentation d'imposer des diktats.

Point n'est besoin de souligner que la réalité du poids des facteurs externes et de la présence militaire non seulement conditionne notre présent mais en même temps oriente le futur à moyen terme. De cet encadrement supranational, force est de reconnaître une très grande diminution de la capacité des principaux protagonistes nationaux et de l'exercice de la souveraineté nationale. Il est intéressant de signaler que pour la première fois, les pays de l'Amérique latine se sont engagés militairement dans un rôle important sur le continent avec un général brésilien à la tête de la force onusienne et un Chilien représentant le secrétaire général des Nations Unies.

De toutes façons nous voulons souligner que la présence actuelle de la MINUSTAH doit contribuer à la normalisation de la vie publique en participant à :

a) *l'indispensable désarmement des gangs armés et à l'établissement de la paix et la sécurité.* En coordination avec les forces de la PNH, les forces de la MINUSTAH doivent arriver à développer une stratégie efficace et continue pour juguler l'insécurité et entreprendre le désarmement des gangs armés, quelles que soient leurs origines maffieuses ou politiques. S'il est vrai que le programme de Démobilisation, Désarmement et Réinsertion (DDR) des ex-militaires, anciens insurgés, a fait beaucoup de bruit et a été proclamé haut et fort, jusqu'à présent il ne s'et pas encore soldé par le succès escompté, de même que la prise des armements qui existent dans le pays.

b) *l'urgente structuration et la professionnalisation d'une vraie police nationale au service de la société.* Cet objectif doit être l'une des priorités de la MINUS-TAH. Tant que la police nationale ne pourra assumer son rôle, il sera difficile pour la nation de récupérer sa pleine et entière responsabilité de la chose publique et d'arriver au retrait programmé des forces militaires.

Pour cela, Il faudra éviter à tout prix les antagonismes inutiles entre la MINUSTAH et la PNH. D'ailleurs toute opération menée ne peut être utile et vraiment réussie que dans la mesure d'une coordination de ces deux forces. Des tâches urgentes s'imposent dans une assistance technique au niveau du recrutement des nouvelles recrues de la PNH (car c'est a partir de là que le bat blesse en grande partie) et la formation indispensable d'une police moderne. Un point important à signaler c'est la nécessité de la diminution des forces militaires au sein de la MINUSTAH et leur remplacement par des policiers.

c) *l'appui technique indispensable pour la réalisation des élections.* Il n'y a pas de doute qu'elle existe. Cependant, elle déborde très souvent son caractère d'appui pour se convertir en instance de décision ou en agissant en dehors des limites techniques. Par ailleurs, les instances parallèles sont tellement multiples qu'il en résulte une cacophonie dans l'action : Nations Unies, OEA, relations bilatérales avec le CEP, l'UNOPS, etc. Il est urgent de préciser les champs de la coopération de chacune de ces instances et aussi leur responsabilité dans l'évolution du processus électoral. D'autant plus que les failles peuvent se multiplier dans les élections immédiatement postérieures.

Une nécessaire redéfinition de la mission et de l'orientation de la MINUS-TAH s'impose dans une perspective de contribution effective au développement économique et social d'Haïti. Se note au sein de la population une certaine irritation qui peut grandir avec la persistance de l'insécurité et la non satisfaction des attentes. Il est vrai que les orientations actuelles de la MINUSTAH devraient se projeter dans la ligne des missions onusiennes de par le monde, avec aussi leur lot de frustrations. Toutefois, dans l'Haïti actuelle, la présence des troupes devrait déboucher en une opération de solidarité d'ample vision susceptible d'accompagner Haïti, nation pionnière de l'émancipation continentale, dans une entreprise de construction, d'institutionnalisation, de développement, de paix durable. Malgré des poches de *no man's land* existantes, Haïti *n'est pas en guerre.* Les sommes considérables dédiées au maintien de la paix devraient s'orienter en grande partie vers la construction de la nation, dans un appui et une aide structurantes.

Dans ce cadre, il faudrait une meilleure *coordination entre les divers pays bailleurs de fonds* pour mettre fin à l'incohérence fréquente des politiques d'aide. Heureusement, cette idée a fait un chemin et les diverses réunions réalisées sur le cas d'Haïti ont mis en exergue cette nécessité.

Une réflexion doit être faite sur la coopération. Traditionnellement, Haïti a bénéficié d'une aide considérable de la communauté internationale, qui s'est révélée peu productive. La crise du système haïtien est aussi dans une certaine mesure la crise d'une façon de demander, de donner et de recevoir l'aide internationale. *Haïti a été un gouffre.* Les grandes sommes de l'aide internationale n'ont pu contribuer au développement et au changement et n'ont pu ou pourront empêcher au sein de la population le découragement et le scepticisme qui constituent à leur tour un frein à la solution des problèmes. Des réussites, bien sûr il y en a eu, mais les frustrations, incompréhensions, inadéquation, dispersion, antagonismes ont marqué l'histoire de cette coopération. Ce constat amène à une vision critique qui ne doit pas seulement se référer à un partenariat difficile mais aussi à la nécessaire recherche d'autres approches, d'autres modalités de coopération. Celle-ci doit rentrer dans une logique qui lui fait éviter, dans un pays pauvre comme Haïti, des dépenses inutiles qui quelquefois frisent le gaspillage et rendent la coopération par conséquent inopérante pour les populations des pays concernés.

Vu la profondeur de la crise haïtienne, la coopération se trouve très souvent dans la situation d'arriver à un *difficile emboîtement de l'humanitaire, de l'urgence, du conjoncturel et du long terme.* Le soulagement ponctuel de la misère (distribution d'aliments, de médicaments, etc.) est factible et a tout son mérite. Cependant, cette politique d'assistance humanitaire, malgré sa pertinence immédiate, revient à réduire la lutte contre la pauvreté au ponctuel, en ignorant ou en projetant dans un avenir lointain tous les autres droits. Considérée ainsi, elle ne saurait empêcher la reproduction de la pauvreté. Lutter contre ce fléau n'est pas seulement soigner les symptômes mais aller aux causes; c'est reconnaître et susciter une participation de la population et une prise en mains à long terme.

Naturellement, on ne manquera pas de parler du rôle clé du Canada parmi les principaux partenaires d'Haïti en matière de développement bilatéral avec une aide multiforme et s'élevant au point de vue financier à 27,50 millions de dollars en 2003–2004. Avec sa politique des 3D, en plus de l'importance de la diaspora haïtienne dans ce pays et la toute récente nomination de Michaëlle Jean, d'origine haïtienne, comme Gouverneure Générale, le Canada marque bien sa politique, appelée à jouer un rôle de plus en plus important en Haïti.

Un point à signaler en parlant de l'internationale : on a tendance a circonscrire les relations d'Haïti avec l'onu ou avec les grandes et moyennes puissances. Cependant, on ne saurait ne pas rappeler ici l'importance des relations avec la République dominicaine, voisin lié à Haïti par la géographie, l'histoire et le développement actuel de notre réalité. La politique adoptée par cette république voisine risque de créer des situations difficiles et de tensions capables de compromettre les relations actuelles et futures entre les deux pays.

Conclusion

La réalité semble mettre en déroute les voix de Cassandres, qui, évoquant la non volonté de ceux qui en ont la charge du pays ou la violence réalisée par certains groupes, annoncent depuis déjà quelque temps, la rentrée de la nation entière dans une dynamique de désintégration aux conséquences incalculables. La stratégie à mettre en place concerne le gouvernement, les partis politiques, la société civile organisée et la communauté internationale.

Il y a déjà quelques décennies, on parlait de « nations non viables ». Aujourd'hui encore, sémantiquement d'autres mots sont utilisés, mais le concept continue à être utilisé. Les notions de nation voyou, s'accompagnent très souvent d'une vision de supériorité raciale ou autre. Il se réfère à une vision statique de l'évolution des nations considérées, en dehors de leur développement historique, de leurs potentialités, de leurs richesses matérielles, de leurs ressources humaines et de leurs perspectives du futur. En plusieurs fois, au cours de cette dernière décade des secteurs étrangers se sont référés à l'établissement d'un protectorat pour Haïti. La tentation est toujours grande d'agir en pro consul dans un pays pauvre, qui a des nécessités immenses et des gouvernants incapables et qui ignorent les intérêts de la nation.

Un fait est certain, les exigences des secteurs conscients de la nation pour la tenue d'élections avec un niveau acceptable de transparence et de participation, soulignent la détermination d'une grande partie de la population à entreprendre cette initiative malgré les risques qu'elle comporte. Elles expriment l'espoir de ce que les conditions pourraient être créées afin de rentrer dans une nouvelle étape de notre vie de peuple. *Elle contient des matériaux pour une avancée vers la modernisation de notre système politique*

Dans le cas d'Haïti, les grandes crises sont indicatrices de la nécessité de grands changements. La situation actuelle exige, à 200 ans de l'indépendance, la construction des bases matérielles, intellectuelles et morales de la nation comme alternative à la misère, la désinstitutionalisation et le désespoir. De la réponse aux défis du présent dépendra le futur. Construire une nation au moment où le pays paraît avoir perdu le train du développement pose la nécessaire ouverture de sentiers originaux correspondant à notre itinéraire passé et à notre situation de sous-développement extrême.

C'est en tirant des leçons de notre expérience de peuple, de la force et la créativité de notre culture, de la compréhension du contenu et des exigences du processus national, que nous aurons la capacité de construire l'Etat-nation, de redéfinir notre identité et de réaliser ce monde de justice, de bien-être, de souveraineté qui a inspiré les combats et les rêves bicentenaires des Haïtiens et des Haïtiennes. C'est le défi que nous autres devons relever avec le concours des nations qui se préoccupent fraternellement du futur de notre pays. Ce ne sera pas facile mais nous autres Haïtiens et Haïtiennes, devons donc nous atteler aujourd'hui a cette tâche gigantesque de recouvrer la dignité, de conquérir la souveraineté et de construire une nation pour tous.

Notes on the **Contributors**

Suzy Castor is a historian and the director of the Centre for Research and Training in Social and Economic Development (CRESFED) in Port-au-Prince. From 1968–1984 (during the Duvalier dictatorships) she was a professor and researcher at the National Autonomous University (UNAM) in Mexico, during which she was made a member of the prestigious National System of Researchers of the Mexican Academy of Sciences. She has published more than fifty articles in journals and edited volumes and has taught at universities in Mexico, the United States, Martinique, Guadeloupe, the Dominican Republic, and Grenada.

Terry Copp is Professor Emeritus and director of the Laurier Centre for Military Strategic and Disarmament Studies at Wilfrid Laurier University. He is the author or co-author of thirteen books and numerous articles on the history of the Canadian Forces. He is the founding editor of the journal *Canadian Military History*, a regular columnist for *Legion Magazine* and the *Kitchener-Waterloo Record*, and chair of the Education Committee of the Canadian Battlefields Foundation. He has recently held a number of workshops and conferences exploring the role of the Canadian military in current international affairs.

Carlo Dade is the senior policy advisor with the Canadian Foundation for the Americas (FOCAL), where he manages programs in transnationalism, corporate social responsibility, and Afro-descendants in the Americas. Prior to joining FOCAL, Mr. Dade was representative for the Dominican Republic, Haiti, and the English-speaking Caribbean at the Inter-American Foundation (IAF), a US government foreign aid agency. He has worked with numerous US, Canadian, and Caribbean government agencies on remittance and Diaspora outreach policies and program development and organized the first conference on the role of the Canadian Diaspora in the development of Haiti.

John English has long been recognized as one of Canada's leading experts on international affairs. Holding a doctorate from Harvard University, he is a senior professor of history and political science at the University of Waterloo. Between 1993 and 1997, he served as a Liberal Member of Parliament. Subsequently, he served as a Special Ambassador for Landmines and as a Special Envoy for the election of Canada to the Security Council. He has also served as president of the Canadian Institute of International Affairs; and is currently the executive director of the Centre for International Governance Innovation, Canada's largest think tank devoted exclusively to the study of international affairs.

Robert Fatton, Jr. is the Julia A. Cooper Professor of Government and Foreign Affairs in the Department of Politics at the University of Virginia. He is the author of several books and a large number of scholarly articles including *Haiti's Predatory Republic: The Unending Transition to Democracy* (2002). He is currently working on a new book tentatively entitled "The Authoritarian Habitus," which seeks to explain the historical and material roots of despotic regimes in Haiti. Born and raised in Port-au-Prince, Fatton studied in France in the mid-1970s, later earning a doctorate from the University of Notre Dame, Indiana.

Jim Hodgson is the Caribbean/Central America program co-ordinator in the national office of The United Church of Canada. He is a journalist and adult educator who worked in the Dominican Republic in the late 1980s and in Mexico from 1994 to 2000. In 1990 he travelled to Haiti as an election observer with a delegation from the Caribbean Conference of Churches, and has visited the country many times from 1984 to the present.

Robert E. Maguire holds a joint appointment at Trinity University in Washington, DC, as director of programs in International Affairs and assistant professor and chair of the International Affairs Program. He is also director of the Trinity University Haiti Program. He has been involved with Haiti since the mid-1970s through work at the Inter-American Foundation, the Department of State, and Johns Hopkins, Brown, and Georgetown universities, and has published extensively on Haiti in the areas of economic and grassroots development, governance, security, international involvement, state/civil society relations.

Colonel Jacques Morneau presently serves as the director of strategic studies at Canadian Forces College in Toronto. From January to July 2005 he served as the Commander for the United Nations Task Force in Port-au-Prince and Chief of Staff of MINUSTAH in Haiti. Prior to this he held many important posts including director of staff at Regional Headquarters Allied Forces North Europe and Senior Canadian Officer in Burnssum, The Netherlands, from April 2000 until December 2003. Col. Morneau holds a master's degree in International Studies from King's College London and attended the Royal College of Defence Studies in London, UK, in 2003.

Yasmine Shamsie is an assistant professor in the Department of Political Science at Wilfrid Laurier University where she teaches Latin American politics and international relations. She specializes in the political economy of democracy promotion with a focus on the inter-American system. Her research has focused on OAS peacebuilding efforts in Haiti and its conflict prevention work in Guatemala. She is a Fellow at the Centre for Research on Latin America and the Caribbean (CERLAC) at York University.

Andrew S. Thompson holds a Ph.D. in history from the University of Waterloo in Waterloo, Canada, and has written on questions of human rights and international governance. In March-April 2004, he was the media officer for an Amnesty International human rights lobbying and fact-finding mission to Haiti.